SIMPLE
KETO

SIMPLE KETO

13-Digit ISBN: 978-1-64643-349-0
10-Digit ISBN: 1-64643-349-1

This book may be ordered by mail from the publisher.
Please include $5.99 for postage and handling.
Please support your local bookseller first!

Books published by Cider Mill Press Book Publishers are available at special discounts for bulk purchases in the United States by corporations, institutions, and other organizations. For more information, please contact the publisher.

Cider Mill Press Book Publishers
"Where good books are ready for press"
PO Box 454
12 Spring Street
Kennebunkport, Maine 04046

Visit us online!
cidermillpress.com

Typography: Dunbar Low, Acumin Pro

Image Credits: Pages 24–25, 28–29, 40–41, 44–45, 55, 60, 68, 76–77, 86–87, 98–99, 104–105, 116, 119, 148, 168–169, 202, 205, 209, 210, 213, 214, 217, 221, 222, 225, and 230–231 used under official license from Shutterstock.com.

Cover and page 151 courtesy of StockFood.

All other images courtesy of Cider Mill Press.

Printed in China

Front cover image: Chipotle Rib Eye, see page 150
Front endpaper image: Asian Beef Salad, see page 164
Back endpaper image: Seafood Salad, see page 146

1 2 3 4 5 6 7 8 9 0
First Edition

SIMPLE
KETO

OVER 100 QUICK & EASY
LOW-CARB, HIGH-FAT RECIPES

CIDER MILL
PRESS

BOOK
PUBLISHERS
KENNEBUNKPORT, MAINE

CONTENTS

INTRODUCTION

The ketogenic diet goes by many names—low-carb, high fat (LCHF), low-carb, keto—but at its heart the concept remains the same: deprive your body of carbs so it can turn to fat and stored body fat for energy, taking advantage of a process called "ketosis."

Normally, our bodies use glucose as their primary source of energy, derived through the carbohydrates we eat. On the keto diet, we deprive our body of these carbs by limiting consumption of them to under 20 to 30 grams in a day, or roughly 5 percent of our total intake of food. When this happens, our body has to find an alternate source of fuel to keep us going, and that is where ketosis kicks in. The liver converts fatty acids into ketone bodies that the brain and other organs can use as fuel.

Keto effectively turns your body into a fat-burning machine, making it a great way to lose weight, while also lowering your overall body fat. But you don't need to have a weight problem to be following the keto diet—a lot of people find that it gives them greater mental clarity, lowers cholesterol and blood pressure, and keeps them away from the processed and sugar-heavy foods that are now believed to be at the root of many diseases.

The keto diet has also been known to be very effective in helping people who suffer from diabetes, epilepsy, and a number of autoimmune diseases. In fact, keto is not new—it was actually formulated for epilepsy patients and was found to greatly reduce the frequency and intensity of seizures. We're just now realizing the many other benefits that come from the keto lifestyle.

But all of these benefits don't come easy. To succeed with keto, one has to keep a close watch over how much protein, fat, and carbs one has consumed each day, as well as break a number of detrimental habits that have inevitably become ingrained over one's pre-keto life. You'll have to keep tabs on your "macros," short for "macronutrients," which is the nutritional breakdown of the components of your food. These include carbohydrates, proteins, and fats—the three components that you must keep track of on keto.

Macros can be tracked through fitness apps like MyFitnessPal or Lose It!. On a keto diet, it's important to monitor your daily macros, to ensure you're getting just enough of your daily calories from fat sources. Twenty to 25 percent of your fat macros should come from protein, and 5 to 10 percent from carbohydrates, specifically net carbs. This will keep your body in ketosis and fat-burning mode.

What are net carbs, you ask? Most foods containing carbs have a dietary fiber or roughage component. Fiber is important for the body, because it helps with the absorption of nutrients in your gut and regulates bowel movements. A lot of dietary fiber is also insoluble and passes through your gut without being digested, so it doesn't count towards your total carb intake. Simply put, net carbs are the total amount of carbs in your food, minus the fiber. On keto, you want to keep your net carb intake between 5 to 10 percent of your daily calories.

When it comes to consuming carbs on the keto diet, you want those to come largely from vegetables, specifically green, leafy vegetables like spinach, kale, lettuce, chard, etc. Cruciferous vegetables like cauliflower and broccoli are high in fiber, and zucchini and eggplant are also sources of good carbs. You want to avoid starchy vegetables like potatoes, sweet potatoes, and corn—these are likely to kick you out of ketosis with just a mouthful. More colorful vegetables like peppers, tomatoes, and red onions can be consumed, but they're best eaten in moderation. It's also possible that some of your carbs might come from dairy products like cheese, so you want to read labels for those carefully. All grains and grain products are off the table. You want to be especially careful with store-bought sauces and even mayonnaise—it's amazing how many hidden carbs they can have.

Apart from the vegetables mentioned earlier, there is a whole lot to eat on the keto diet. When it comes to protein sources, you can pretty much eat any kind of meat. This includes poultry like chicken, duck, turkey, and quail; red meats like beef, lamb, pork, and venison; and also eggs of all kinds. High-fat dairy products like cream, cheese, butter, and full-fat yogurt (in moderation) are all keto-friendly, though you want to avoid milk itself as its carb count is high. Nuts are a great source of good fats, especially macadamia nuts, hazelnuts, almonds, and walnuts, but you want to be careful about eating peanuts and carb-heavy cashews in large quantities. That is why tracking macros and keeping tabs on your overall carb intake is so important.

Now, since sugar is completely off the table on keto, it eliminates most fruits from the diet. However, there are a few that fall into the keto-friendly category—mainly avocados, and berries such as strawberries, raspberries, and blackberries. Once again, it's important to consume these in moderation in keeping with your macros.

Fats, the largest component of your diet, can come from both plant and animal sources. When choosing meat, choose fattier cuts, and eat poultry with the skin on, since that's where a lot of the fat is. The other sources of pure fat are your oils, healthy ones like olive, coconut, and avocado, as well as ghee and butter. Animal fats like lard, bacon grease, and duck fat are not only healthy, but also add some serious flavor to your food.

As you can see from the decadent list of foods mentioned above, keto is not synonymous with deprivation, like most diets. It's not magic. And it's not easy to keep yourself on track. But this book will help keep things simple, and keep your focus on what you need to do to keep feeling better than you ever have before.

BREAKFAST

Keto-friendly breakfast foods are a great way to start the day—so great, in fact, that it seems silly to limit them to a particular time frame. In truth, these recipes are all substantial enough to give you a lift whenever you need one, and carry the additional benefit of brief prep times, meaning that when you need to keep both your health and your day on track, you can confidently turn here.

SERVINGS: 4
(1 SERVING = 1 PANCAKE)

PREP TIME: 5 MINUTES

COOKING TIME: 15 MINUTES

NUTRITIONAL INFO:
(PER SERVING)

CALORIES: 266
FAT: 23 G

NET CARBS: 3 G
PROTEIN: 10 G

ALMOND FLOUR PANCAKES

INGREDIENTS

1.75 oz. cream cheese

1.75 oz. heavy cream

2 eggs

1 teaspoon pure vanilla extract

3.5 oz. almond flour

½ teaspoon baking powder

Pinch of kosher salt

1 teaspoon pumpkin spice mix
(optional)

2 to 3 drops of liquid stevia,
powdered erythritol, or other
keto-friendly sweetener

1 strawberry, hulled and sliced,
for garnish

Unsalted butter, for serving

Sugar-free maple syrup,
for serving

1   Place the cream cheese in a microwave-safe bowl and microwave it on medium for 30 seconds. Remove the cream cheese from the microwave, add the heavy cream, and stir until combined. Let the mixture cool.

2   Add the eggs and vanilla and stir until thoroughly combined. Add the remaining ingredients, except for those designated for garnish or for serving, and stir until combined.

3   Warm a nonstick skillet over medium heat and coat it with nonstick cooking spray. Ladle ¼-cup portions of the batter into the skillet and cook until the edges are set and the bottoms are browned, about 2 minutes. For fluffier pancakes, cover the skillet as they cook. Turn the pancakes over and cook until cooked through, another 2 minutes. Garnish with the strawberry and serve with butter and maple syrup.

SERVINGS: 5
(1 SERVING = 1 PANCAKE)

PREP TIME: 5 MINUTES

COOKING TIME: 20 MINUTES

NUTRITIONAL INFO:
(PER SERVING)

CALORIES: 221
FAT: 18 G

NET CARBS: 3 G
PROTEIN: 6 G

COCONUT FLOUR PANCAKES

INGREDIENTS

¾ oz. coconut flour

½ teaspoon baking powder

½ teaspoon cinnamon

Pinch of kosher salt

1.75 oz. unsalted butter,
plus more for serving

1.75 oz. cream cheese

1.75 oz. heavy cream

3 eggs

½ teaspoon pure vanilla extract

2 to 3 drops liquid stevia
or preferred keto-friendly
sweetener

Sugar-free maple syrup,
for serving (optional)

Fresh berries, for serving
(optional)

Sugar-free whipped cream,
for serving (optional)

1   Sift the coconut flour, baking powder, cinnamon, and salt into a mixing bowl, stir to combine, and set the mixture aside.

2   Place the butter and cream cheese in a microwave-safe bowl and microwave on medium for 30 seconds. Remove the bowl from the microwave, add the cream, and whisk until combined. Let the mixture cool slightly. Once the mixture has cooled slightly, stir in the eggs, vanilla, and sweetener.

3   Add the dry mixture to the wet mixture and whisk until it comes together as a smooth batter.

4   Place a nonstick skillet over medium heat and coat it with nonstick cooking spray. Ladle ¼-cup portions of the batter into the skillet, cover it, and cook until the edges of the pancakes are set and the bottoms are browned, about 2 minutes. Flip the pancakes over and cook until cooked through, another 2 minutes. Serve with maple syrup and butter or fresh berries and whipped cream.

NUTRITIONAL INFO:
(PER SERVING)

CALORIES: 586

FAT: 52 G

NET CARBS: 8 G

PROTEIN: 13 G

ALMOND FLOUR WAFFLES

INGREDIENTS

1.75 oz. almond flour

¾ oz. cheddar cheese, grated

¼ cup heavy cream

½ teaspoon baking powder

¼ teaspoon kosher salt

2 to 3 drops of liquid stevia or preferred keto-friendly sweetener

1 egg

Sugar-free maple syrup, for serving

Unsalted butter, for serving

1   Preheat a waffle iron and coat it with nonstick cooking spray. Place all of the ingredients, except for the maple syrup and butter, in a bowl and whisk until the mixture comes together as a smooth batter.

2   Working in batches, pour the batter into the waffle iron and cook the waffles until they are crispy and golden brown, 2 to 3 minutes. Serve with syrup and butter and enjoy.

NUTRITIONAL INFO:
(PER SERVING)

CALORIES: 481
FAT: 43 G

NET CARBS: 7 G
PROTEIN: 18 G

PEANUT BUTTER WAFFLES

INGREDIENTS

2.8 oz. natural, no sugar added peanut butter

2 tablespoons unsalted butter, plus more for serving

1.4 oz. cream cheese

1.4 oz. heavy cream

½ teaspoon baking powder

Stevia or preferred keto-friendly sweetener, to taste

2 eggs

Sugar-free maple syrup, for serving

1   Preheat a waffle iron and coat it with nonstick cooking spray. Place the peanut butter, butter, and cream cheese in a microwave-safe bowl and microwave on medium for 30 seconds. Remove, add the cream, baking powder, and sweetener, and stir until the mixture is well combined.

2   Add the eggs and whisk until the mixture comes together as a smooth, thick batter. Working in batches, ladle the batter into the waffle iron and cook until the waffles are crispy and golden brown, 2 to 3 minutes. Serve with the sugar-free maple syrup and additional butter.

NUTRITIONAL INFO:
(PER SERVING)

CALORIES: 226
FAT: 21 G

NET CARBS: 3 G
PROTEIN: 7 G

LEMON POPPY SEED MUFFINS

INGREDIENTS

4.9 oz. almond flour

1½ tablespoons poppy seeds

½ teaspoon baking powder

Salt, to taste

Zest and juice of 1 lemon

3 oz. unsalted butter

3.5 oz. preferred keto-friendly sweetener

3 oz. sour cream

½ teaspoon pure vanilla extract

2 eggs

1 Preheat the oven to 350°F and line 8 wells of a muffin pan with paper wrappers. Place the almond flour, poppy seeds, baking powder, salt, and lemon zest in a mixing bowl and stir to combine. Set the mixture aside.

2 Place the butter and sweetener in the work bowl of a stand mixer fitted with the paddle attachment and beat the mixture until it is pale and fluffy. If using a granulated sweetener, pulse it 3 or 4 times in the blender before adding it to the butter so that it has an easier time dissolving.

3 Add the sour cream to the butter mixture and beat until incorporated. Add the vanilla, eggs, and lemon juice, beat until they have been incorporated, and then add the dry mixture. Beat the mixture until it comes together as a smooth batter. Divide the batter among the wrappers, filling each one two-thirds of the way.

4 Place the muffins in the oven and bake until they are golden brown and a toothpick inserted into the center of each one comes out clean, about 25 minutes. Remove the muffins from the oven and let them cool in the pan for 20 minutes before enjoying.

SERVINGS: 4   **PREP TIME:** 10 MINUTES   **COOKING TIME:** 20 MINUTES

NUTRITIONAL INFO:
(PER SERVING)

CALORIES: 351   **NET CARBS:** 4 G
FAT: 27 G   **PROTEIN:** 21 G

CORNED BEEF & CAULIFLOWER HASH

INGREDIENTS

3 tablespoons unsalted butter

¼ cup finely diced onion

2 cups diced cauliflower florets

1 garlic clove, minced

¼ cup chicken broth

16 oz. corned beef, shredded

Salt and pepper, to taste

1 Place the butter in a large skillet and melt it over medium-high heat. Add the onion and cauliflower and cook, stirring frequently, until the onion starts to brown, about 6 minutes. Stir in the garlic and cook, stirring continually, for 1 minute.

2 Add the chicken broth and cook until the cauliflower is tender and the liquid has evaporated, about 10 minutes.

3 Stir in the corned beef and cook until it is warmed through, about 3 minutes. Season the hash with salt and pepper and enjoy.

SERVINGS: 1   **PREP TIME:** 5 MINUTES   **COOKING TIME:** 5 MINUTES

NUTRITIONAL INFO:
(PER SERVING)

CALORIES: 97
FAT: 8 G

NET CARBS: 1 G
PROTEIN: 3 G

VIETNAMESE EGG COFFEE

INGREDIENTS

1 egg yolk

1 tablespoon heavy cream

1½ teaspoons pure vanilla extract

Stevia or preferred keto-friendly sweetener, to taste

¼ cup freshly brewed espresso

1   Place the egg yolk, cream, vanilla, and sweetener in a mixing bowl and whisk until the mixture is pale and foamy.

2   Pour the espresso into a mug, add the egg cream, gently stir, and enjoy.

VIETNAMESE EGG COFFEE SEE PAGE 23

NUTRITIONAL INFO:
(PER SERVING)　　　　**CALORIES:** 368　　　　**NET CARBS:** 1 G
　　　　　　　　　　　FAT: 32 G　　　　　　　**PROTEIN:** 17 G

BACON & CHEESE OMELET

INGREDIENTS

2 slices of bacon, chopped

1 egg

Salt and pepper, to taste

1 tablespoon chopped
fresh basil

1 tablespoon grated
cheddar cheese

1 Place the bacon in a small skillet and cook it over medium heat, stirring occasionally, until it is browned and crispy, about 6 minutes.

2 Whisk the egg until it is scrambled, season it with salt and pepper, and add it to the skillet. Cook, undisturbed, until the bottom of the egg starts to set, 3 to 4 minutes.

3 Sprinkle the basil and cheese over the egg and fold the omelet. Turn off the heat, cover the pan, and let the omelet sit until the egg is just cooked through and the cheese has melted. Enjoy immediately.

NUTRITIONAL INFO:
(PER SERVING)

CALORIES: 282
FAT: 22 G

NET CARBS: 4 G
PROTEIN: 15 G

BELL PEPPER & BROCCOLI FRITTATA

INGREDIENTS

2 tablespoons extra-virgin olive oil

¼ cup chopped onion

½ bell pepper, sliced thin

¾ cup chopped broccoli florets

2 garlic cloves, minced

8 large eggs

¼ cup heavy cream

2 tablespoons chopped fresh parsley

1 tablespoon fresh thyme

1 Preheat the oven to 350°F. Place the olive oil in a large cast-iron skillet and warm it over medium heat. Add the onion, bell pepper, and broccoli and cook, stirring frequently, until the vegetables start to brown, about 8 minutes. Add the garlic and cook, stirring continually, for 1 minute.

2 Place the eggs, cream, and fresh herbs in a mixing bowl and whisk to combine. Add the egg mixture to the skillet and shake the pan to ensure that it is evenly distributed.

3 Place the skillet in the oven and bake the frittata until it is set and the top is lightly browned, 6 to 10 minutes.

4 Remove the skillet from the oven and let it sit for 10 minutes before serving.

BELL PEPPER & BROCCOLI FRITTATA, SEE PAGE 27

NUTRITIONAL INFO: **CALORIES:** 360   **NET CARBS:** 1 G
(PER SERVING)   **FAT:** 34 G   **PROTEIN:** 13 G

BROWN BUTTER SCRAMBLED EGGS

INGREDIENTS

2 eggs

2 tablespoons unsalted butter

Salt and pepper, to taste

Fresh chives, diced, for garnish

Keto-friendly bread, for serving
(optional)

1   Scramble the eggs in a bowl and set them aside.

2   Place the butter in a medium skillet and cook it over medium
    heat until it starts to brown. Reduce the heat to the lowest setting,
    add the eggs, and cook, stirring occasionally, until they are set,
    about 3 minutes.

3   Season the eggs with salt and pepper, garnish with the chives, and
    serve with a slice of keto-friendly bread, if desired.

NUTRITIONAL INFO:
(PER SERVING)

CALORIES: 241

FAT: 22 G

NET CARBS: 1 G

PROTEIN: 10 G

CHEESY FRIED EGGS

INGREDIENTS

1 tablespoon unsalted butter

1 egg

½ oz. cheddar cheese, grated

Salt and pepper, to taste

1 Place the butter in a skillet and melt it over medium heat.

2 Crack the egg into the pan, top it with the cheese, and season it with salt and pepper. Reduce the heat to low, cover the pan, and cook until the egg white is set and the yolk has firmed up, about 2 minutes. Enjoy immediately.

NUTRITIONAL INFO:
(PER SERVING)

CALORIES: 732
FAT: 58 G

NET CARBS: 5 G
PROTEIN: 33 G

EGG & SAUSAGE SANDWICH

INGREDIENTS

3.5 oz. ground pork

¼ teaspoon smoked paprika

¼ teaspoon dried oregano

Salt and pepper, to taste

1½ teaspoons unsalted butter, plus more to taste

1 slice of American cheese

1 egg

Coconut Flour Mug Bread (see page 65)

1 Place the ground pork, paprika, and oregano in a bowl, season the mixture with salt and pepper, and stir to combine. Using your hands, form the mixture into a patty.

2 Place half of the butter in a skillet and melt it over medium heat. Place the patty in the skillet and cook until it is completely cooked through, about 5 minutes per side.

3 Place the cheese on the patty, cover the pan, and cook until it is melted. Remove the patty from the pan and cover it loosely with aluminum foil.

4 Place the remaining butter in the pan. When it has melted, add the egg, prick the yolk, and fry until it has been cooked through. Slice the bread, butter it, and toast it in the pan. Assemble the sandwich and enjoy immediately.

NUTRITIONAL INFO:
(PER SERVING)

CALORIES: 301

FAT: 26 G

NET CARBS: 1 G

PROTEIN: 9.5 G

EGGS BENEDICT

INGREDIENTS

1.4 oz. unsalted butter, melted

½ portion of Mug Bread
(see page 57)

1 slice of ham

½ teaspoon fresh lemon juice

½ egg yolk

Salt and pepper, to taste

1 egg

Fresh chives, chopped,
for garnish

1　Spread some of the butter on both sides of the bread. Place a skillet over medium heat and toast the bread in it. Add the ham to the pan and cook until it has browned, about 3 minutes.

2　Bring an inch of water to a simmer in a saucepan. Bring water to a boil in another saucepan. Place the lemon juice and egg yolk in a heatproof mixing bowl and whisk to combine. Place the bowl over the simmering water and gradually add the remaining melted butter, whisking continually. When the hollandaise sauce has thickened, season it with salt and pepper and remove the pan from heat. Leave the bowl over the saucepan to keep the sauce warm.

3　Reduce the heat beneath the other saucepan and crack the egg into the water. Poach until the white is set, about 3 minutes, and remove the egg with a slotted spoon.

4　Place the ham and then the egg on top of the bread. Spoon the hollandaise over the top and garnish with the chives.

TIP: In the event that your hollandaise sauce separates while the egg is poaching, take a warm bowl, add 1 tablespoon hot water, and slowly whisk it into the broken hollandaise until it comes together again.

SERVINGS: 6 **PREP TIME:** 10 MINUTES **COOKING TIME:** 35 MINUTES

NUTRITIONAL INFO:
(PER SERVING)

CALORIES: 243

FAT: 17.6 G

NET CARBS: 2.5 G

PROTEIN: 17.7 G

FRITTATA BITES

INGREDIENTS

2 tablespoons extra-virgin olive oil

8 oz. cremini mushrooms, quartered

12 large eggs

⅔ cup unsweetened almond milk

¾ oz. Parmesan cheese, grated

½ teaspoon kosher salt

¼ teaspoon black pepper

1 red bell pepper, stem and seeds removed, diced

2 tablespoons fresh thyme

2 tablespoons chopped fresh chives

1. Preheat the oven to 350°F. Line a 6-well muffin pan with paper wrappers. Place the olive oil in a skillet and warm it over medium heat. Add the mushrooms and cook, stirring occasionally, until they start to brown, about 6 minutes. Remove the pan from heat.

2. Place the eggs, almond milk, Parmesan, salt, and black pepper in a mixing bowl and stir to combine. Stir in the bell pepper, and then divide the mixture among the paper wrappers.

3. Place the pan in the oven and bake the frittatas until they are set, golden brown, and puffy, about 20 minutes.

4. Remove the frittatas from the oven and let them cool briefly before sprinkling the herbs over the top and serving.

GOLDEN MILK

INGREDIENTS

2⅓ cups unsweetened
almond milk

2 teaspoons fresh turmeric root,
peeled and grated

1 teaspoon ground turmeric,
plus more for garnish

⅛ teaspoon ground ginger

⅛ teaspoon cinnamon

3 cardamom pods,
lightly crushed

1 teaspoon stevia or preferred
keto-friendly sweetener

1 Place ¼ cup of the almond milk, the turmeric root, ground turmeric, ground ginger, cinnamon, and cardamom pods in a saucepan and warm the mixture over medium heat, stirring occasionally, until it is a smooth paste.

2 Whisk in 1¾ cups of the almond milk while pouring it in a slow, steady stream. Bring the mixture to a simmer and cook until it is warmed through, 3 to 4 minutes, making sure it does not come to a boil. Strain the milk into each of the serving glasses and stir the sweetener into each serving.

3 Pour the remaining almond milk into a small saucepan and bring it to a simmer over medium heat. Froth it with a milk frother and spoon it on top of each beverage. Dust each beverage with additional ground turmeric and enjoy.

GOLDEN MILK, SEE PAGE 39

NUTRITIONAL INFO:
(PER SERVING)

CALORIES: 358

FAT: 29.7 G

NET CARBS: 4.9 G

PROTEIN: 12.1 G

ORANGE CHIA PUDDING WITH PISTACHIOS

INGREDIENTS

2 cups coconut milk

2 cups unsweetened almond milk

1.4 oz. white chia seeds

1.4 oz. plus 1 tablespoon black chia seeds

1 tablespoon stevia or preferred keto-friendly sweetener

½ teaspoon orange blossom water

Juice of ½ orange

1.75 oz. chopped unsalted pistachios

1 Place the coconut milk, almond milk, white chia seeds, 1.4 oz. of the black chia seeds, sweetener, and orange blossom water in a mixing bowl and stir to combine. Cover the bowl with plastic wrap and refrigerate the pudding overnight.

2 Stir the orange juice into the pudding. Divide it among the serving bowls and sprinkle the pistachios and remaining black chia seeds on top of each portion.

NUTRITIONAL INFO:
(PER SERVING)

CALORIES: 296

FAT: 18.5 G

NET CARBS: 7.2 G

PROTEIN: 12.9 G

CHOCOLATE CHIA PUDDING

INGREDIENTS

5.6 oz. chia seeds

2½ cups unsweetened almond milk

2 tablespoons stevia or preferred keto-friendly sweetener

1.2 oz. unsweetened cacao powder

¼ cup full-fat Greek yogurt

¾ oz. blueberries

1 oz. blackberries

1 tablespoon sugar-free bittersweet chocolate

1   Place the chia seeds, almond milk, and sweetener in a mixing bowl and stir to combine. Cover the bowl and let the mixture sit at room temperature for 30 minutes.

2   Stir the mixture and then sift the cacao powder over it while stirring continually. Divide the mixture among four serving glasses, cover them with plastic wrap, and refrigerate them overnight.

3   Top each serving with some of the yogurt, berries, and chocolate and enjoy.

CHOCOLATE CHIA PUDDING, SEE PAGE 43

NUTRITIONAL INFO:
(PER SERVING)

CALORIES: 516

FAT: 43 G

NET CARBS: 3 G

PROTEIN: 28 G

HAM & MUSHROOM OMELET

INGREDIENTS

3 eggs

Salt, to taste

¼ teaspoon black pepper

½ teaspoon cayenne pepper

½ teaspoon dried oregano

2 tablespoons heavy cream

¾ oz. Swiss cheese, grated

1 tablespoon unsalted butter

1 tablespoon extra-virgin olive oil

¾ oz. button mushrooms, diced

¾ oz. leftover ham, diced

1   Place the eggs, salt, pepper, cayenne, and oregano in a bowl and whisk until combined. Stir the cream and cheese into the mixture.

2   Place half of the butter and half of the olive oil in a skillet and warm it over medium heat. Add the mushrooms and cook, stirring frequently, until they release their liquid, about 3 minutes. Add the ham and cook until the mixture starts to brown, about 8 minutes.

3   Reduce the heat to medium-low, remove the pan from heat, add the remaining butter and olive oil, and then pour in the egg mixture. Swirl the pan to distribute it evenly, place it back on the burner, cover the pan, and cook until the egg is set, 1 to 2 minutes. Fold one half of the omelet over the other, cover the pan, and let the omelet sit until the egg is just cooked through. Enjoy immediately.

NUTRITIONAL INFO:
(PER SERVING)

CALORIES: 430

FAT: 41 G

NET CARBS: 1 G

PROTEIN: 13 G

PESTO SCRAMBLED EGGS

INGREDIENTS

2 eggs

1 tablespoon heavy cream

1 tablespoon Pesto
(see page 85)

1 tablespoon unsalted butter

Salt and pepper, to taste

1   Crack the eggs into a bowl, add the cream and Pesto, and whisk until the mixture is combined.

2   Place the butter in a skillet and melt it over medium heat. Reduce the heat to the lowest setting, add the eggs, and cook until they are set, about 5 minutes. Season the eggs with salt and pepper and enjoy.

NUTRITIONAL INFO:
(PER SERVING)

CALORIES: 504
FAT: 40 G

NET CARBS: 2 G
PROTEIN: 31 G

PIZZA OMELET

INGREDIENTS

3 eggs

Salt and pepper, to taste

Pinch of cayenne pepper

Pinch of finely chopped
fresh parsley

2 teaspoons extra-virgin olive oil

¾ oz. pepperoni or salami, sliced

½ oz. white mushrooms, sliced

1 oz. mozzarella or cheddar
cheese, grated

1   Place the eggs, salt, pepper, cayenne pepper, and parsley in a bowl and whisk until combined.

2   Place the olive oil in a cast-iron skillet and warm it over medium heat. Add the egg mixture and top it with the pepperoni, mushrooms, and cheese. Place the skillet in the oven, turn on the broiler, and cook until the eggs are set and the cheese has melted, 5 to 7 minutes.

3   Remove the skillet from the oven and let the omelet cool slightly before enjoying.

BREADS, SIDES & SNACKS

The process of transforming one's health via the ketogenic diet means that you have to leave so much behind: carb-laden loaves of bread, decadent, starchy sides, and those irresistible, nutrient-vacant snacks. But that doesn't mean these categories are completely out of the question on keto. They just need to be tweaked slightly, transformed into foods that help you achieve your wellness goals, rather than set you back in your pursuit. Filled with fiber and plenty of flavor, the recipes in this section will help you round out your table, keep things fresh, and make sure you remain on track.

SERVINGS: 8　　　　**PREP TIME:** 10 MINUTES　　　　**COOKING TIME:** 35 MINUTES

NUTRITIONAL INFO:
(PER SERVING)

CALORIES: 61

FAT: 4.9 G

NET CARBS: 0.6 G

PROTEIN: 3.7 G

CLOUD BREAD

INGREDIENTS

4 large eggs, yolks and whites separated

¼ cup cream cheese, softened

Pinch of kosher salt

¼ teaspoon cream of tartar

1　Preheat the oven to 300°F. Place the egg yolks and cream cheese in a mixing bowl and beat the mixture until it is smooth.

2　Place the egg whites, salt, and cream of tartar in a separate bowl and whip the mixture until it holds soft, fluffy peaks. Fold the meringue into the egg yolk mixture.

3　Coat two large baking sheets with nonstick cooking spray. Spoon 8 mounds of the batter onto the sheets, leaving plenty of space between each mound.

4　Place the baking sheets in the oven and bake until the slices of bread are golden brown, about 35 minutes.

5　Remove the bread from the oven and let it cool on the baking sheets before enjoying.

SERVINGS: 1

PREP TIME: 2 MINUTES

COOKING TIME: 2 MINUTES

NUTRITIONAL INFO:
(PER SERVING)

CALORIES: 324

FAT: 28 G

NET CARBS: 2 G

PROTEIN: 13 G

MUG BREAD

INGREDIENTS

1 oz. almond flour

½ oz. extra-virgin olive oil

½ teaspoon baking powder

1 egg

1. Place all of the ingredients in a large mug and stir to combine.
2. Place the mug in the microwave and microwave on medium for 1½ minutes. Remove, turn the mug over, and tap the bottom of it until the bread slides out.

NUTRITIONAL INFO:
(PER SERVING)

CALORIES: 324
FAT: 28 G

NET CARBS: 2 G
PROTEIN: 13 G

BREAD CRUMBS

INGREDIENTS

1 portion of Mug Bread
(see page 57)

1 Preheat the oven to 245°F. Slice the bread, place the slices on a baking sheet, and place them in the oven. Bake until they are dry and crumbly, 1 to 2 hours.

2 Remove the slices of bread from the oven and let them cool completely. Place them in a food processor and blitz until they are broken down into bread crumbs. Store in an airtight container until ready to use.

NUTRITIONAL INFO:
(PER SERVING)

CALORIES: 41
FAT: 2 G

NET CARBS: 0.7 G
PROTEIN: 3.9 G

KETO WRAPS

INGREDIENTS

8 large egg whites

1 oz. coconut flour

⅔ cup water

¼ teaspoon baking powder

¼ teaspoon kosher salt

½ oz. fresh mint leaves, chopped

1 tablespoon extra-virgin olive oil

1   Place all of the ingredients, except for the olive oil, in a mixing bowl and stir until the mixture comes together as a smooth batter.

2   Coat the bottom of a cast-iron skillet with some of the olive oil and warm it over medium heat. When the oil starts to shimmer, ladle a small amount of the batter into the pan and tilt the pan to coat the surface entirely. Cook until the bottom of the wrap is set and golden brown, 2 to 3 minutes. Flip the wrap over and cook for another minute.

3   Transfer the cooked wrap to a plate, cover it with aluminum foil, and repeat the process until all of the wraps have been cooked.

SERVINGS: 12
(1 SERVING = 1 SLICE)

PREP TIME: 10 MINUTES

COOKING TIME: 50 MINUTES

NUTRITIONAL INFO:
(PER SERVING)

CALORIES: 174
FAT: 15 G

NET CARBS: 2 G
PROTEIN: 7 G

COCONUT FLOUR BREAD

INGREDIENTS

2.6 oz. coconut flour

1 teaspoon xanthan gum

½ oz. psyllium husk

1 teaspoon baking powder

½ teaspoon kosher salt

6 eggs

6 tablespoons extra-virgin olive oil

½ cup warm water (110°F)

1 Preheat the oven to 335°F. Line a 9 x 5–inch loaf pan with parchment paper and coat it with nonstick cooking spray.

2 Place the coconut flour, xanthan gum, psyllium husk, baking powder, and salt in a bowl and stir to combine. In another bowl, whisk together the eggs and olive oil. Working in three increments, add the dry mixture to the wet mixture and incorporate each portion thoroughly before adding the next. Add the water and whisk until the mixture comes together as a smooth batter.

3 Pour the batter into the loaf pan, place it in the oven, and bake until a toothpick inserted into the center of the loaf comes out clean, about 40 minutes.

4 Remove the bread from the oven and let it cool before removing it from the pan.

NUTRITIONAL INFO:
(PER SERVING)

CALORIES: 286

FAT: 24 G

NET CARBS: 4 G

PROTEIN: 8 G

COCONUT FLOUR MUG BREAD

INGREDIENTS

1 oz. coconut flour

1 tablespoon heavy cream

1 tablespoon extra-virgin olive oil

1 egg

¼ teaspoon baking powder

Salt, to taste

1 Place all of the ingredients in a large mug and stir until thoroughly combined.

2 Place the mug in the microwave and microwave on medium for 1½ minutes. Remove the mug, turn it over, and tap the bottom of the mug until the bread slides out.

SERVINGS: 6
(1 SERVING = 1 ROLL)

PREP TIME: 10 MINUTES

COOKING TIME: 15 MINUTES

NUTRITIONAL INFO:
(PER SERVING)

CALORIES: 141
FAT: 13 G

NET CARBS: 1 G
PROTEIN: 4 G

DINNER ROLLS

INGREDIENTS

1.75 oz. cream cheese

1 oz. extra-virgin olive oil

1.75 oz. almond flour

½ teaspoon baking powder

Salt, to taste

2 eggs, yolks and whites separated

¼ teaspoon cream of tartar

1   Preheat the oven to 355°F and coat 6 wells of a muffin pan with nonstick cooking spray. Place the cream cheese in a microwave-safe bowl and microwave it on medium for 30 seconds. Remove the cream cheese from the microwave, stir in the olive oil, and then add the almond flour, baking powder, and salt. Stir until well combined and let the mixture cool slightly. Whisk in the egg yolks and set the mixture aside.

2   Place the egg whites and cream of tartar in a separate bowl and whisk until the mixture holds stiff peaks. Working in three increments, fold the egg white mixture into the cream cheese mixture.

3   Pour the mixture into the muffin pan, place it in the oven, and bake until the rolls are puffy and golden brown, 12 to 15 minutes. Remove the rolls from the oven and let them cool briefly before serving.

SERVINGS: 20 (1 SERVING = 1 SLICE)	PREP TIME: 10 MINUTES	COOKING TIME: 40 MINUTES

NUTRITIONAL INFO: (PER SERVING)	CALORIES: 86 FAT: 7 G	NET CARBS: 2 G PROTEIN: 4 G

PEANUT BUTTER BREAD

INGREDIENTS

8.8 oz. natural, no sugar added peanut butter

3 eggs

1 teaspoon white vinegar

½ teaspoon baking soda

Stevia or preferred keto-friendly sweetener, to taste

Pinch of kosher salt

1   Preheat the oven to 335°F and coat a 9 x 5–inch loaf pan with nonstick cooking spray. Place all of the ingredients in a mixing bowl and work the mixture until it comes together as a smooth dough.

2   Place the dough in the loaf pan, place it in the oven, and bake until a toothpick inserted into the center of the bread comes out clean, about 25 minutes.

3   Remove the bread from the oven and let it cool briefly before slicing.

TIP: This dough is quite thick and sticky and can be hard to work with, but it comes together with a bit of elbow grease and patience.

NUTRITIONAL INFO:
(PER SERVING)

CALORIES: 159
FAT: 11 G

NET CARBS: 4 G
PROTEIN: 10 G

CAULIFLOWER HAMBURGER BUNS

INGREDIENTS

8.8 oz. cauliflower florets

Salt and pepper, to taste

2 tablespoons freshly grated Parmesan cheese

2 tablespoons cream cheese, softened

1 egg

1 Preheat the oven to 375°F. Place the cauliflower florets in a food processor and pulse until they acquire a couscous-like consistency.

2 Place the cauliflower in a microwave-safe bowl and microwave on medium until tender, 5 to 7 minutes. Place the cauliflower in a kitchen towel and wring the towel to remove as much liquid from the cauliflower as possible.

3 Place 6.3 oz. of the cauliflower in a mixing bowl, season it with salt and pepper, and then stir in the Parmesan, cream cheese, and egg. Divide the mixture into four portions, place them on a parchment-lined baking sheet, and shape them into buns.

4 Place the buns in the oven and bake until fully cooked through and golden brown, about 20 minutes.

5 Remove the buns from the oven and serve immediately.

NUTRITIONAL INFO:
(PER SERVING)

CALORIES: 88

FAT: 8 G

NET CARBS: 1 G

PROTEIN: 4 G

FATHEAD CRACKERS

INGREDIENTS

3.5 oz. mozzarella cheese, grated

1.4 oz. cream cheese

Salt and pepper, to taste

1 tablespoon chopped fresh parsley

1.75 oz. almond flour

1 Preheat the oven to 390°F and line a baking sheet with parchment paper. Place the mozzarella and cream cheese in a microwave-safe bowl and microwave on medium until the mozzarella has melted, about 1 minute.

2 Remove the mixture from the microwave and stir it with a rubber spatula. Stir in the salt, pepper, and parsley, add the almond flour, and knead the mixture until it comes together as a smooth dough.

3 Place the dough between two sheets of parchment paper and roll it out into a thin rectangle.

4 Place the dough on the baking sheet, place it in the oven, and bake until it is golden brown, about 10 minutes.

5 Remove the large cracker from the oven, transfer it to a wire rack, and cut it into the desired shapes when it has cooled slightly.

NUTRITIONAL INFO:
(PER SERVING)   **CALORIES:** 173   **NET CARBS:** 4 G
FAT: 14.4 G   **PROTEIN:** 5.3 G

MULTISEED CRACKERS

INGREDIENTS

3.75 oz. sesame seeds

1.3 oz. golden linseeds

2.3 oz. shelled sunflower seeds

3 tablespoons pumpkin seeds

2 tablespoons flaxseeds

2 tablespoons chopped almonds

1⅔ cups water

1½ teaspoons kosher salt

3 tablespoons coconut oil, melted

1 Preheat the oven to 225°F. Line a large baking sheet with parchment paper. Place the seeds, almonds, and water in a large bowl, stir, and let the mixture stand for 20 minutes.

2 Whisk in the salt and set the mixture aside.

3 Coat the parchment paper with a little bit of the coconut oil. Spread the mixture on the baking sheet in a thin, even layer. Brush the top with the remaining coconut oil, place the pan in the oven, and bake for 1 hour and 45 minutes.

4 Remove the pan from the oven, carefully flip the large cracker over, and peel away the parchment paper. Return the pan to the oven and bake for another 1 hour and 45 minutes.

5 Remove the pan from the oven and let the large cracker cool for 10 minutes before cutting smaller, round crackers from it. Let the crackers cool completely on wire racks before enjoying.

SERVINGS: 4   **PREP TIME:** 5 MINUTES   **COOKING TIME:** 10 MINUTES

NUTRITIONAL INFO:
(PER SERVING)

CALORIES: 63
FAT: 4.1 G

NET CARBS: 2.2 G
PROTEIN: 2.2 G

CAULIFLOWER RICE

INGREDIENTS

1 medium head of cauliflower, trimmed

1 tablespoon extra-virgin olive oil

Salt and pepper, to taste

1   Cut the head of cauliflower into chunks, place them in a food processor, and blitz until they are rice-like in consistency.

2   Place the olive oil in a large skillet and warm it over medium heat. Add the cauliflower, season it with salt and pepper, and cook, stirring occasionally, until the cauliflower is tender and lightly golden brown, 6 to 8 minutes.

CAULIFLOWER RICE SEE PAGE 75

SERVINGS: 4

PREP TIME: 5 MINUTES

COOKING TIME: 10 MINUTES

NUTRITIONAL INFO: (PER SERVING)

CALORIES: 162

FAT: 15 G

NET CARBS: 3 G

PROTEIN: 3 G

CAULIFLOWER MASH

INGREDIENTS

Salt and pepper, to taste

8 oz. cauliflower florets

1.75 oz. unsalted butter

1.75 oz. heavy cream

1. Bring salted water to a boil in a medium saucepan. Add the cauliflower and cook until it is tender, about 7 minutes.
2. Drain the cauliflower and place it in a food processor along with the butter, cream, salt, and pepper. Blitz until the mixture is a rich, smooth puree and enjoy immediately.

NUTRITIONAL INFO:
(PER SERVING)

CALORIES: 328

FAT: 29 G

NET CARBS: 3 G

PROTEIN: 14 G

CHEESY BACON SLAW

INGREDIENTS

3.5 oz. bacon, chopped

5.3 oz. cabbage, shredded

Salt and pepper, to taste

¼ teaspoon paprika

½ teaspoon dried oregano

1 oz. cheddar cheese, grated

1.75 oz. heavy cream

Fresh parsley, finely chopped, for garnish

1 Place the bacon in a skillet and cook, stirring occasionally, over medium heat until it is crispy, about 8 minutes.

2 Add the cabbage to the pan and season the mixture with salt, pepper, the paprika, and oregano. As the cabbage becomes tender, stir in the cheese and cream. When the cabbage is cooked to your liking, remove the pan from heat, garnish the dish with fresh parsley, and enjoy.

NUTRITIONAL INFO:
(PER SERVING)

CALORIES: 71
FAT: 7 G

NET CARBS: 1 G
PROTEIN: 1 G

MARINARA SAUCE

INGREDIENTS

2 tablespoons extra-virgin olive oil

1.75 oz. red onion, diced

Salt and pepper, to taste

2 garlic cloves, minced

Red pepper flakes, to taste

1 (14 oz.) can of diced tomatoes, with their liquid

1 handful of fresh basil, chopped

5 tablespoons chopped fresh oregano

1 tablespoon unsalted butter

1   Place the olive oil in a small saucepan and warm it over medium heat. Add the onion, season it with salt, and cook, stirring occasionally, until the onion is translucent, about 3 minutes.

2   Stir in the garlic, season the mixture with the red pepper flakes, and cook, stirring continually, for 2 minutes. Stir in the tomatoes, season the sauce with salt and pepper, cover the pan, and cook until the oil rises to the top of the sauce, 10 to 12 minutes.

3   Stir in the basil and oregano and cook for another 2 minutes. Stir in the butter and enjoy.

SERVINGS: 7
(1 SERVING = 1 TABLESPOON)

PREP TIME: 5 MINUTES

COOKING TIME: 15 MINUTES

NUTRITIONAL INFO:
(PER SERVING)

CALORIES: 25
FAT: 2 G

NET CARBS: 1 G
PROTEIN: 1 G

KETCHUP

INGREDIENTS

2 garlic cloves, chopped

10.6 oz. tomatoes, chopped

1 tablespoon unsalted butter

¼ teaspoon kosher salt

¼ teaspoon white pepper

¼ teaspoon cayenne pepper

¼ teaspoon smoked paprika

1 tablespoon white vinegar

1 teaspoon soy sauce

2 drops of liquid stevia or preferred keto-friendly sweetener

1. Place the garlic and tomatoes in a blender and puree until smooth. Strain the puree to remove any seeds and pieces of skin. Set the puree aside.

2. Place the butter in a medium saucepan and melt it over medium heat. Add the tomato puree and cook for 5 to 7 minutes, stirring continually.

3. Add the remaining ingredients and cook, stirring occasionally, until the mixture has thickened to the desired consistency.

4. Remove the pan from heat and let the ketchup cool before serving or storing in the refrigerator.

NUTRITIONAL INFO:
(PER SERVING)

CALORIES: 142
FAT: 16 G

NET CARBS: 0 G
PROTEIN: 2 G

PESTO

INGREDIENTS

1 oz. Parmesan cheese, grated

¾ oz. pine nuts

2 garlic cloves, minced

1 oz. fresh parsley

1.75 oz. fresh basil

¾ cup extra-virgin olive oil

1½ teaspoons fresh lemon juice

Salt, to taste

1   Place the Parmesan, pine nuts, garlic, parsley, and basil in a food processor and puree until smooth.

2   Place the puree in a bowl and gradually add the olive oil while whisking continually. Stir in the lemon juice, season the pesto with salt, and use as desired.

PESTO, SEE PAGE 85

NUTRITIONAL INFO:
(PER SERVING)

CALORIES: 25
FAT: 2 G

NET CARBS: 1 G
PROTEIN: 0 G

BARBECUE SAUCE

INGREDIENTS

1.75 oz. unsalted butter

2.8 oz. onion, chopped

½ oz. garlic cloves, chopped

1 teaspoon kosher salt

1 teaspoon black pepper

1 teaspoon paprika

1 teaspoon cayenne pepper

1 teaspoon cumin

5.3 oz. tomatoes, diced

1 teaspoon balsamic vinegar

1 teaspoon stevia or preferred
keto-friendly sweetener

1 teaspoon Worcestershire sauce

1 tablespoon yellow mustard

2.1 oz. apple cider vinegar

1 tablespoon sriracha

1   Place the butter in a small saucepan and melt it over low heat. Add the onion and garlic and cook, stirring frequently, until the onion starts to soften, about 5 minutes. Add the salt, pepper, paprika, cayenne, and cumin and cook, stirring continually, for 2 minutes.

2   Add the tomatoes, balsamic vinegar, sweetener, and Worcestershire sauce. Cover the pan and cook the sauce for 7 to 8 minutes.

3   Using an immersion blender or a food processor, puree the sauce until it is smooth.

4   Return the sauce to the saucepan, stir in the mustard, apple cider vinegar, and sriracha, and cook until the sauce thickens slightly, about 5 minutes. Use immediately or store in the refrigerator until ready to use.

NUTRITIONAL INFO: CALORIES: 28   NET CARBS: 3 G
(PER SERVING)   FAT: 22 G   PROTEIN: 18 G

BOLOGNESE SAUCE

INGREDIENTS

1 tablespoon extra-virgin olive oil

1 tablespoon unsalted butter

1.75 oz. red onion, grated

8.8 oz. ground beef

8.8 oz. ground pork

Salt and pepper, to taste

Red pepper flakes, to taste

Dried oregano, to taste

1 teaspoon fresh thyme

2 garlic cloves, minced

3.5 oz. white mushrooms, chopped

3.5 oz. tomatoes, diced

1.75 oz. water

1 beef or chicken bouillon cube

3.5 oz. baby spinach

3.5 oz. heavy cream

1 tablespoon chopped fresh parsley

1   Place the olive oil and butter in a large skillet and warm the mixture over medium heat. Add the red onion and cook, stirring occasionally, until it is translucent, about 3 minutes.

2   Add the beef and pork and cook, breaking up the meats with a wooden spoon. Season the mixture with salt, pepper, red pepper flakes, and oregano and cook for 2 to 3 minutes.

3   Stir in the thyme and garlic and cook until the meat starts to brown.

4   Add the mushrooms, tomatoes, water, and bouillon cube, stir to incorporate, and cover the pan. Simmer the sauce for 15 minutes, checking occasionally to see that there is enough liquid in the pan to keep everything from burning. If the pan starts to look dry, add more water.

5   Stir in the spinach, cover the pan, and cook until the spinach has wilted, 1 to 2 minutes. Stir in the cream and parsley, cook until the sauce is warmed through, and serve.

CREAMED SPINACH

INGREDIENTS

1 tablespoon extra-virgin olive oil

3.5 oz. spinach

Salt and pepper, to taste

⅛ teaspoon freshly grated nutmeg

2 teaspoons unsalted butter

¾ oz. Parmesan cheese, grated

2 tablespoons heavy cream

1   Place the olive oil in a large skillet and warm it over medium heat. Add the spinach, season it with salt and pepper, stir in the nutmeg, and cook until the spinach has wilted, 2 to 3 minutes.

2   Stir in the butter, Parmesan, and cream, cook for 1 minute or until everything is warmed through, and serve.

NUTRITIONAL INFO:
(PER SERVING)

CALORIES: 250

FAT: 22 G

NET CARBS: 5 G

PROTEIN: 10 G

SAUTÉED MUSHROOMS

INGREDIENTS

1 tablespoon extra-virgin olive oil

3.5 oz. white mushrooms, sliced

1.75 oz. oyster mushrooms, chopped

Salt and pepper, to taste

1 tablespoon unsalted butter

1 sprig of fresh rosemary

1 garlic clove, minced

1   Place the olive oil in a large skillet and warm it over medium heat. Add the mushrooms, season them with salt and pepper, and cook for 3 minutes. Add half of the butter and the rosemary and cook until the mushrooms release their liquid, 6 to 8 minutes.

2   Add the garlic and cook, stirring continually, for 1 minute. Turn off the heat, stir in the remaining butter, and serve.

NUTRITIONAL INFO: **CALORIES:** 373   **NET CARBS:** 14.5 G
(PER SERVING)   **FAT:** 26.3 G   **PROTEIN:** 15.8 G

SOUR CREAM & BACON CAULIFLOWER TART

INGREDIENTS

Pinch of kosher salt, plus more to taste

8 oz. cauliflower florets

1 egg, beaten

⅓ cup goat cheese, softened

2 tablespoons cornstarch

2 tablespoons extra-virgin olive oil

1 cup sour cream

6 slices of bacon, chopped

1 red onion, sliced thin

Black pepper, to taste

1   Preheat the oven to 400°F. Line a large baking sheet with parchment paper and spray it with nonstick cooking spray. Bring salted water to a boil in a large saucepan. Place the cauliflower florets in a food processor and pulse until they are rice-like in texture. Add them to the boiling water, cover the pan, and cook the cauliflower until it is tender, 4 to 5 minutes.

2   Drain the cauliflower and place it in a kitchen towel. Wring the towel to remove as much liquid from the cauliflower as possible, and then place the cauliflower in a bowl. Add the egg, goat cheese, and cornstarch, season with salt, and stir until the mixture just starts holding together.

3   Place the mixture on the baking sheet and shape it into a large oval. Brush the top with the olive oil, place the pan in the oven, and bake until the tart is golden brown and dry to the touch, about 35 minutes. Remove the tart from the oven, spread the sour cream over the top, and sprinkle the bacon over it. Return the tart to the oven and bake until the bacon is crispy, about 10 minutes.

4   Remove the tart from the oven, top it with the onion, and season with salt and pepper. Let the tart cool briefly before serving.

NUTRITIONAL INFO:
(PER SERVING)

CALORIES: 281

FAT: 28.6 G

NET CARBS: 3.7 G

PROTEIN: 2.6 G

ASPARAGUS WITH EGG SAUCE

INGREDIENTS

12 asparagus spears, trimmed

½ cup full-fat Greek yogurt

½ cup mayonnaise

2 tablespoons fresh lemon juice

½ teaspoon kosher salt

⅛ teaspoon black pepper

¼ cup warm water (110°F)

2 poached eggs

2 tablespoons extra-virgin olive oil

2 oz. fresh parsley, chopped

1   Bring water to a boil in a saucepan and prepare an ice water bath. Add the asparagus to the boiling water and cook until just tender to the tip of a knife, about 2 minutes. Transfer to the ice water bath, let it sit for 2 minutes, and then drain. Pat the asparagus dry with paper towels and set it aside.

2   Place the yogurt, mayonnaise, lemon juice, salt, pepper, and water in a bowl and stir to combine. Chop one of the poached eggs and fold it into the sauce.

3   Place the olive oil in a skillet and warm over high heat. When the oil starts to shimmer, add the asparagus and cook, while stirring, until it starts to brown all over, about 2 minutes.

4   Top the asparagus with the sauce and remaining poached egg and sprinkle the parsley over the dish.

ASPARAGUS WITH EGG SAUCE, SEE PAGE 97

NUTRITIONAL INFO:
(PER SERVING)

CALORIES: 330
FAT: 22 G

NET CARBS: 1 G
PROTEIN: 30 G

BACON BOMBS

INGREDIENTS

8.8 oz. ground pork

2 garlic cloves, minced

1 teaspoon chopped
fresh rosemary

½ teaspoon five-spice powder

½ teaspoon cayenne pepper

Salt and pepper, to taste

3.5 oz. mozzarella cheese,
cubed

8.8 oz. bacon

Parmesan cheese, grated,
for garnish

Fresh parsley, chopped,
for garnish

1   Preheat the oven to 400°F. Place the pork, garlic, rosemary, five-spice powder, cayenne pepper, salt, and pepper in a bowl and stir to combine. Divide the mixture into 1.75-oz. portions, place a cube of mozzarella on top of each, and form the pork mixture into meatballs around the cheese.

2   Wrap a slice of bacon around each meatball, place them on a baking sheet, and place them in the oven. Bake until the meatballs are cooked through and the bacon is crispy, about 20 minutes.

3   Remove the meatballs from the oven, garnish with grated Parmesan and parsley, and enjoy.

NUTRITIONAL INFO:
(PER SERVING)

CALORIES: 337

FAT: 26.3 G

NET CARBS: 2.1 G

PROTEIN: 21.7 G

ZUCCHINI ROLL-UPS

INGREDIENTS

2 zucchini, sliced very thin lengthwise

3 tablespoons extra-virgin olive oil

1 teaspoon fennel seeds

2 cups ground pork

1 shallot, minced

2 garlic cloves, minced

¼ cup crumbled feta cheese

¾ teaspoon kosher salt

¼ teaspoon black pepper

1   Place the slices of zucchini on paper towels and let them sit for 15 minutes to dry out. Pat them dry with paper towels, place them on a baking sheet, and brush them all over with 2 tablespoons of the olive oil. Place the slices of zucchini in the oven and broil until they are browned on both sides, about 6 minutes. Remove from the oven and let them cool.

2   Place the remaining olive oil in a skillet and warm it over medium heat. Add the fennel seeds and cook, stirring continually, for 30 seconds. Add the pork, raise the heat to medium-high, and cook, while breaking up the pork with a wooden spoon, until it is starting to brown, about 6 minutes.

3   Stir in the shallot and garlic, reduce the heat to medium, and cook until the pork is completely cooked through, about 3 minutes.

4   Remove the pan from heat and stir in the feta, salt, and pepper. Spoon the mixture over the slices of zucchini, roll them up, and secure them with toothpicks.

NUTRITIONAL INFO: CALORIES: 83   NET CARBS: 2.2 G
(PER SERVING)   FAT: 7.3 G   PROTEIN: 1.2 G

KALE CRISPS

INGREDIENTS

7 oz. kale leaves

2 tablespoons extra-virgin olive oil

1 teaspoon flaky sea salt

1   Preheat the oven to 225°F. Rinse the kale and pat it dry with paper towels. Tear the leaves into large pieces, making sure to remove and discard any thick stems. Place the kale in a mixing bowl, add the oil and salt, and toss until the kale is evenly coated.

2   Arrange the kale leaves on two baking sheets, place them in the oven, and bake for 15 minutes. Rotate the baking sheets and bake until the kale is crispy, about 10 minutes.

3   Remove the kale crisps from the oven and let them cool briefly before enjoying.

KALE CRISPS, SEE PAGE 103

NUTRITIONAL INFO:
(PER SERVING)

CALORIES: 150
FAT: 14 G

NET CARBS: 3 G
PROTEIN: 2 G

CAULIFLOWER HUMMUS

INGREDIENTS

Salt and pepper, to taste

17.6 oz. cauliflower, chopped

2.1 oz. tahini paste

3 garlic cloves, minced

½ cup extra-virgin olive oil

3.5 oz. Kalamata olives, pits removed, plus more for garnish

1 teaspoon paprika

1 teaspoon cumin

Juice of 1 lemon

1 Bring salted water to a boil in a large saucepan. Add the cauliflower and cook until it is tender, about 10 minutes.

2 Drain the cauliflower, place it in a food processor, add the tahini, garlic, olive oil, olives, paprika, cumin, and lemon juice, and season the mixture with salt and pepper. Blitz until the mixture is very smooth and garnish with more olives.

NUTRITIONAL INFO:
(PER SERVING)

CALORIES: 157
FAT: 7 G

NET CARBS: 3 G
PROTEIN: 21 G

POT STICKERS

INGREDIENTS

25 cabbage leaves

17.6 oz. ground chicken

¾ oz. onion, grated

½ teaspoon mashed ginger

½ teaspoon mashed garlic

½ scallion, chopped

2 tablespoons chopped
fresh cilantro

1 tablespoon sesame oil

Salt and pepper, to taste

Dipping Sauce (see sidebar),
for serving

1   Bring water to a boil in a large saucepan. Place the cabbage in the water and boil until tender, 8 to 10 minutes. Drain the cabbage and let it cool.

2   Combine the remaining ingredients, except for the Dipping Sauce, in a bowl and set the mixture aside.

3   Divide the chicken mixture into ten 1.75-oz. portions and place each one in a cabbage leaf. Wrap the leaf tightly around the filling to create a dumpling. Line a steaming tray with the remaining cabbage leaves and place the dumplings in the tray.

4   Bring an inch of water to a boil in a saucepan. Place the steaming tray over the water and steam until the chicken is cooked through, about 10 minutes.

5   Place the steamed dumplings in a skillet and cook over medium heat until browned on both sides, 1 to 2 minutes per side. Serve with the Dipping Sauce.

DIPPING SAUCE

Place 1 teaspoon natural, no sugar added peanut butter, 1 teaspoon sriracha, 1 teaspoon extra-virgin olive oil, ½ teaspoon soy sauce, ½ teaspoon rice vinegar, the juice of ½ lime, ¼ teaspoon mashed ginger, and ¼ teaspoon mashed garlic in a mixing bowl, season the mixture with salt, and stir until thoroughly combined. This recipe will make 2 servings of sauce; the macros per serving are as follows: 43 calories, 4 grams fat, 2 grams net carbs, and 1 gram protein.

SERVINGS: 6   **PREP TIME:** 5 MINUTES   **COOKING TIME:** 20 MINUTES

NUTRITIONAL INFO:
(PER SERVING)

CALORIES: 202   **NET CARBS:** 3.6 G
FAT: 13.8 G   **PROTEIN:** 13.2 G

DEVILED EGGS

INGREDIENTS

12 large eggs

½ cup mayonnaise

2 teaspoons Dijon mustard

1 tablespoon capers, chopped

1 teaspoon caper brine

2 tablespoons chopped
sun-dried tomatoes in olive oil,
drained

1 tablespoon extra-virgin olive oil

½ teaspoon kosher salt

¼ teaspoon black pepper

¼ cup fresh parsley, chopped,
for garnish

1 Place the eggs in a large saucepan and cover by 2 inches with cold water. Bring it to a boil, reduce the heat, and simmer the eggs for 10 minutes. Drain and rinse the eggs under cold water for 2 minutes.

2 Crack and peel the eggs, rinsing off any shell. Carefully slice the eggs in half, remove the yolks, and place them in a mixing bowl. Mash the yolks with a fork and set the halved egg whites aside.

3 Add the mayonnaise, mustard, capers, caper brine, sun-dried tomatoes, olive oil, salt, and pepper to the mashed yolks and stir until thoroughly combined. Spoon the mixture into the cavities in the egg white halves, garnish with the parsley, and enjoy.

NUTRITIONAL INFO:
(PER SERVING)

CALORIES: 263
FAT: 12 G

NET CARBS: 1 G
PROTEIN: 35 G

GARLIC & PARMESAN CHICKEN WINGS

INGREDIENTS

9 full chicken wings, separated into drumette and flat

1 teaspoon kosher salt

½ teaspoon black pepper

½ teaspoon cayenne pepper

1 teaspoon smoked paprika

1 teaspoon dried oregano

1 tablespoon unsalted butter, melted

1 teaspoon fresh lemon juice

1 tablespoon keto-friendly hot sauce

4 garlic cloves, minced

1 teaspoon chopped fresh parsley

1.75 oz. Parmesan cheese, grated

1 Preheat the oven to 375°F and set a wire rack in a rimmed baking sheet. Season the wings with the salt, pepper, cayenne, paprika, oregano, butter, and lemon juice, place them on the wire rack, and place them in the oven. Bake the wings until they are golden brown, about 20 minutes. Remove the wings and raise the oven's temperature to 400°F.

2 Combine the remaining ingredients in a bowl and then toss the chicken wings in the mixture. Place them back on the wire rack and bake until they are cooked through and the cheese has melted, about 10 minutes.

3 Remove the wings from the oven and enjoy immediately.

NUTRITIONAL INFO:
(PER SERVING)

CALORIES: 166
FAT: 9 G

NET CARBS: 0 G
PROTEIN: 20 G

BUFFALO WINGS

INGREDIENTS

1 teaspoon kosher salt

1 teaspoon black pepper

1 teaspoon paprika

3.5 oz. keto-friendly hot sauce

36 oz. chicken wings, separated
into drumette and flat

1.75 oz. unsalted butter

¾ oz. cream cheese

1   Preheat the oven to 400°F and set a wire rack in a rimmed baking sheet. Place the salt, pepper, paprika, and half of the hot sauce in a bowl and stir to combine. Add the chicken wings and let them marinate for about 10 minutes.

2   Place the wings on the wire rack in the baking sheet, place them in the oven, and bake until the wings are cooked through, about 25 minutes. Remove the wings from the oven and let them cool slightly.

3   Place the butter and cream cheese in a microwave-safe bowl and microwave on medium until the butter has melted, about 30 seconds. Add the remaining hot sauce to the mixture and stir until thoroughly combined. Toss the wings in the sauce and serve immediately.

NUTRITIONAL INFO:
(PER SERVING)

CALORIES: 103

FAT: 5 G

NET CARBS: 2 G

PROTEIN: 11 G

CHICKEN SATAY WINGS

INGREDIENTS

1 tablespoon natural, no sugar added peanut butter

1 oz. coconut cream

5 teaspoons soy sauce

1 tablespoon rice vinegar

2 teaspoons sriracha

2 teaspoons fish sauce

Salt and pepper, to taste

½ teaspoon ground ginger

½ teaspoon garlic powder

17.6 oz. chicken wings, separated into drumette and flat

¼ teaspoon black sesame seeds

¼ teaspoon white sesame seeds

Keto-friendly hot sauce, for serving

1   Place the peanut butter, coconut cream, soy sauce, vinegar, sriracha, fish sauce, salt, pepper, ginger, and garlic powder in a bowl and stir to combine. Add the chicken wings and toss until they are evenly coated. Let the chicken wings marinate for 1 hour.

2   Preheat the oven to 410°F and set a wire rack in a rimmed baking sheet. Sprinkle the sesame seeds over the chicken wings, place them on the wire rack, and bake until they are golden brown and cooked through, about 25 minutes.

3   Remove the wings from the oven and serve with hot sauce.

NUTRITIONAL INFO:
(PER SERVING)

CALORIES: 282
FAT: 27 G

NET CARBS: 6.9 G
PROTEIN: 2.8 G

ZUCCHINI FALAFEL

INGREDIENTS

7 oz. canned chickpeas,
drained and rinsed

1 small zucchini, grated

2 garlic cloves, minced

½ oz. finely chopped
fresh parsley

4 oz. finely chopped
fresh cilantro

1½ teaspoons baking powder

3 tablespoons coconut flour,
plus more as needed

Salt and pepper, to taste

4 cups canola oil

1   Place the chickpeas, zucchini, garlic, and herbs in a food processor and pulse until the mixture is a rough puree.

2   Transfer to a mixing bowl, add the baking powder and coconut flour, and work the mixture with your hands until it is a smooth, nonsticky dough. Incorporate more coconut flour as needed if the dough is not quite holding together.

3   Season the dough with salt and pepper, form the dough into golf ball-sized spheres, and set them aside.

4   Place the oil in a Dutch oven and warm it to 350°F. Working in batches of three or four, add the falafel to the oil and fry until they are golden brown, 3 to 4 minutes. Transfer the cooked falafel to a paper towel-lined plate to drain and tent with aluminum foil to keep them warm.

NUTRITIONAL INFO: **CALORIES:** 140   **NET CARBS:** 2.1 G
(PER SERVING)   **FAT:** 12.8 G   **PROTEIN:** 2.8 G

CAULIFLOWER FRITTERS

INGREDIENTS

For the Fritters

6.5 oz. cauliflower florets

⅓ cup cream cheese, softened

¼ cup plus 2 tablespoons coconut flour

2 tablespoons flaxseed meal

2 large eggs, lightly beaten

1 teaspoon dried basil

½ teaspoon kosher salt

¼ teaspoon black pepper

⅓ cup avocado oil

For the Dip

⅓ cup mayonnaise

⅓ cup full-fat Greek yogurt

⅓ cup cream cheese, softened

2 tablespoons chopped fresh basil

¼ teaspoon kosher salt

¼ teaspoon black pepper

¼ cup warm water (110°F)

1   To begin preparations for the fritters, bring 2 inches of water to a simmer in a saucepan. Place the cauliflower florets in a food processor and blitz until they are rice-like in consistency. Place the cauliflower in a steaming tray, place the tray above the simmering water, and steam the cauliflower until it is just tender, 3 to 4 minutes. Transfer the cauliflower to a large mixing bowl and let it cool for 5 minutes.

2   Add the cream cheese, 2 tablespoons of coconut flour, flaxseed meal, eggs, dried basil, salt, and pepper to the bowl and stir until combined. Scoop ¼-cup portions of the mixture onto parchment-lined baking sheets and press down on the fritters until they are flat. Place the baking sheets in the refrigerator for 30 minutes.

3   Dust the fritters with the remaining coconut flour. Place the oil in a large skillet and warm it over medium heat. Working in batches of three or four, place the fritters in the oil and fry until they are golden brown all over, about 3 minutes per side. Place the cooked fritters on a paper towel–lined plate and cover loosely with aluminum foil to keep warm.

4   To prepare the dip, place all of the ingredients in a bowl and stir to combine. Serve alongside the fritters.

SERVINGS: 8
(1 SERVING = 2.4 OZ.)

PREP TIME: 15 MINUTES

COOKING TIME: 20 MINUTES

NUTRITIONAL INFO:
(PER SERVING)

CALORIES: 95
FAT: 7 G

NET CARBS: 4 G
PROTEIN: 2 G

BABA GHANOUSH

INGREDIENTS

17.6 oz. eggplant

2 garlic cloves, diced

1.75 oz. tahini paste

½ teaspoon fresh lemon juice

1 teaspoon kosher salt

½ teaspoon cumin

½ teaspoon paprika

¼ teaspoon cayenne pepper

2 tablespoons extra-virgin olive oil

1 tablespoon chopped fresh parsley, for garnish

1   Poke holes in the eggplant and roast it over an open flame or in a 400°F oven until it is charred and has collapsed, about 20 minutes. Let the eggplant cool and then peel off the skin. Don't worry if a few bits of charred skin remain.

2   Roughly chop the roasted eggplant, place it in a bowl, and stir in the garlic, tahini, lemon juice, seasonings, and half of the olive oil.

3   Drizzle the remaining olive oil over the dish, garnish with the parsley, and enjoy.

ENTREES

Your experience with the keto diet will largely center around your encounters with the recipes featured in this chapter. These are the meals that your each and every day will point toward, those that promise to be satisfying enough that you can say no to all of the temptation that inevitably occurs during the day, and packed with enough nutrition that you can be confident you are giving your body precisely what it needs to remain in ketosis. It's a lot to ask of a single preparation, but these entrees are more than able to meet the call.

BACON-WRAPPED MEATLOAF

INGREDIENTS

17.6 oz. ground pork

Salt, to taste

1½ teaspoons black pepper

1 tablespoon paprika

1½ teaspoons cayenne pepper

2 tablespoons Italian seasoning

1 oz. cheddar cheese, grated

¼ oz. scallion, chopped

⅔ oz. bell pepper, diced

6 slices of bacon

3 tablespoons Barbecue Sauce (see page 88)

1   Season the pork with salt, the pepper, paprika, cayenne, and Italian seasoning.

2   Cover a cutting board with plastic wrap, place the pork on it, and form it into a rectangle. In the center of the rectangle, arrange the cheese, scallion, and bell pepper. Roll the pork up into a loaf and cover it tightly with plastic wrap. Chill the pork in the refrigerator for 30 minutes.

3   Preheat the oven to 390°F. Set a wire rack in a rimmed baking sheet.

4   Arrange the bacon in a rectangle on the cutting board. Place the meatloaf on top of the bacon and wrap the bacon around the meatloaf.

5   Brush the meatloaf with the Barbecue Sauce and place it on the wire rack. Place the meatloaf in the oven and bake until it is cooked through, about 45 minutes.

6   Remove the meatloaf from the oven and let it rest for 10 minutes before slicing and serving.

BOUQUET GARNI

Cut a 4-inch section of kitchen twine. Tie one side of the twine around 2 bay leaves, 3 sprigs of fresh thyme, and 3 sprigs of fresh parsley and knot the twine tightly. To use, attach the other end of the twine to one of the pot's handles and slip the herbs into the broth.

NUTRITIONAL INFO:
(PER SERVING)

CALORIES: 610
FAT: 39 G

NET CARBS: 5 G
PROTEIN: 49 G

BEEF BOURGUIGNON

INGREDIENTS

7 oz. bacon, cubed

35 oz. chuck roast, cubed

Salt and pepper, to taste

5.3 oz. onions, chopped

1 tablespoon unsalted butter

14 oz. white mushrooms, chopped

¼ teaspoon cayenne pepper

2 garlic cloves, minced

1 cup red wine

1 beef bouillon cube

1 Bouquet Garni (see sidebar)

10.6 oz. water

1 tablespoon fresh chives, chopped, for garnish

Sour cream, for garnish

1 Place the bacon in a Dutch oven and cook it over medium heat, stirring occasionally, until it is browned and crispy, 6 to 8 minutes. Using a slotted spoon, transfer the bacon to a bowl and set it aside.

2 Season the beef with salt and pepper, add to the pot, working in batches to avoid crowding the pot, and cook until it is browned all over, turning the beef as needed. Transfer the browned beef to the bowl with the bacon.

3 Add the onions and butter to the pot and cook, stirring occasionally, until they start to brown, about 8 minutes.

4 Add the mushrooms, season them with salt and the cayenne, and cook, stirring occasionally, until they start to brown, about 8 minutes.

5 Add the garlic and cook, stirring continually, for 1 minute. Stir in the wine, bouillon cube, and Bouquet Garni and then return the beef and bacon to the pot, along with any juices.

6 Add the water until the beef is completely covered and bring it to a boil. Cover the pot, reduce the heat to low, and cook until the beef is very tender, about 1½ hours.

7 Remove the Bouquet Garni and discard it. Ladle the stew into warmed bowls and garnish each portion with the chives and a dollop of sour cream.

NUTRITIONAL INFO:
(PER SERVING)

CALORIES: 590

FAT: 43 G

NET CARBS: 6 G

PROTEIN: 50 G

BEEF STROGANOFF

INGREDIENTS

28 oz. chuck roast, cut into long strips

Salt and pepper, to taste

1 tablespoon extra-virgin olive oil

1 tablespoon unsalted butter

3.5 oz. onion, sliced

7 oz. white mushrooms, sliced

1 teaspoon paprika

½ teaspoon cayenne pepper

17.6 oz. water

2.6 oz. sour cream

1.75 oz. heavy cream

Fresh chives, chopped, for garnish

1   Season the beef with salt and pepper. Place the olive oil in a Dutch oven and warm it over medium heat. Working in batches to avoid crowding the pot, add the beef and cook until it is browned all over, turning it as necessary. Transfer the browned beef to a plate and set it aside.

2   Add the butter, onion, and mushrooms to the pot and cook, stirring occasionally, until the vegetables start to brown, about 8 minutes.

3   Season the mixture with salt, pepper, paprika, and cayenne, add the water, and return the beef to the pot. Cover, reduce the heat to low, and cook until the beef is very tender and the liquid has reduced by half or more, about 30 minutes.

4   Stir in the sour cream and cream, ladle the dish into warmed bowls, and garnish with chives.

NUTRITIONAL INFO:
(PER SERVING)   **CALORIES:** 503   **NET CARBS:** 7 G
FAT: 32 G   **PROTEIN:** 39 G

CHILI CON CARNE

INGREDIENTS

7 oz. bacon, chopped or cubed

3.5 oz. onion, chopped

2 garlic cloves, minced

2.6 oz. green bell pepper, chopped

17.6 oz. ground beef

Salt, to taste

1 teaspoon black pepper

1 teaspoon cayenne pepper

1 teaspoon cumin

1 teaspoon paprika

7 oz. tomatoes, pureed

7 oz. white mushrooms, sliced

3.5 oz. spinach

1 beef bouillon cube

17.6 oz. water

Fresh oregano, to taste

Fresh cilantro, chopped, to taste

Sour cream, for serving

Avocado, chopped, for serving

1   Place the bacon in a skillet and cook it over medium heat until the fat has rendered. Add the onion and cook, stirring occasionally, until it has softened and the bacon is crispy, about 6 minutes.

2   Add the garlic and bell pepper and cook, stirring frequently, for 3 minutes. Add the ground beef, season it with salt, and stir in the pepper, cayenne, cumin, and paprika. Cook until the beef is browned all over, breaking it up with a wooden spoon as it cooks.

3   Stir in the tomatoes, mushrooms, and spinach and cook until the spinach starts to wilt, about 2 minutes. Add the bouillon cube and water, bring the chili to a simmer, and cook for 10 minutes.

4   Season the chili with oregano and cilantro and cook until it has reduced slightly. Ladle the chili into warmed bowls and serve with sour cream and avocado.

NUTRITIONAL INFO:
(PER SERVING)

CALORIES: 311
FAT: 16 G

NET CARBS: 7 G
PROTEIN: 30 G

COTTAGE PIE

INGREDIENTS

17.6 oz. cauliflower, chopped

2 egg yolks

1.75 oz. Parmesan cheese, grated, plus more to taste

Salt and pepper, to taste

2 tablespoons unsalted butter

1 tablespoon extra-virgin olive oil

1.75 oz. onion, chopped

2 garlic cloves, minced

17.6 oz. ground beef

1 beef bouillon cube

1 teaspoon Worcestershire sauce

1.75 oz. tomato puree

1½ teaspoons chopped fresh rosemary

½ tablespoon dried thyme

3.5 oz. white mushrooms, diced

3.5 oz. spinach

5.3 oz. water

1 Bring water to a boil in a large saucepan. Add the cauliflower and boil until it is tender, about 8 minutes. Drain and place the cauliflower in a food processor. Blitz until smooth, add the egg yolks and Parmesan, season the mixture with salt and pepper, and blitz until smooth. Set the cauliflower puree aside.

2 Place the butter and olive oil in a large skillet and warm the mixture over medium heat. Add the onion and cook, stirring occasionally, until it is golden brown, 8 to 10 minutes. Add the garlic and cook, stirring continually, for 1 minute.

3 Add the ground beef and cook until it is browned all over, breaking it up with a wooden spoon as it cooks.

4 Stir in the bouillon cube, Worcestershire sauce, tomato puree, rosemary, and thyme and cook for 2 to 3 minutes.

5 Add the mushrooms and spinach, season the mixture with salt and pepper, and cook until the spinach is wilted, about 2 minutes. Add the water and cook for 10 minutes.

6 Transfer the ground beef mixture to a casserole dish, spread the cauliflower puree on top in an even layer, and sprinkle additional Parmesan over the puree. Place the dish in the oven and bake until the top is golden brown, about 15 minutes.

7 Remove the cottage pie from the oven and let it cool briefly before serving.

NUTRITIONAL INFO:
(PER SERVING)

CALORIES: 356

FAT: 30 G

NET CARBS: 8 G

PROTEIN: 10 G

CHEESE & BROCCOLI SOUP

INGREDIENTS

1 tablespoon extra-virgin olive oil

3 tablespoons unsalted butter

1.75 oz. onion, chopped

17.6 oz. broccoli, diced

2 garlic cloves, minced

Salt, to taste

½ teaspoon black pepper

1 teaspoon paprika

½ teaspoon cayenne pepper

17.6 oz. chicken stock, vegetable stock, or water

5.3 oz. heavy cream

3.5 oz. cheddar cheese, grated

1. Place the olive oil and 1 tablespoon of the butter in a medium saucepan and warm the mixture over medium heat. Add the onion and half of the broccoli and cook, stirring occasionally, until the onion starts to brown, about 6 minutes. Add the garlic and cook, stirring continually, for 1 minute.

2. Season the mixture with salt, stir in the pepper, paprika, and cayenne, and cook, stirring continually, for 1 minute. Add the stock or water, cover the pan, and simmer the soup for 5 minutes.

3. Transfer the soup to a food processor and blitz until it is a smooth puree. Set the soup aside.

4. Place the remaining butter in the saucepan and melt it over medium heat. Add the remaining broccoli and cook, without stirring, until it starts to brown, about 5 minutes.

5. Strain the soup back into the saucepan through a fine sieve and bring it to a boil. Reduce the heat so that the soup simmers and cook for 3 to 4 minutes.

6. Stir in the cream and cheese and cook until the cheese has melted. Ladle the soup into warmed bowls and enjoy.

NUTRITIONAL INFO:
(PER SERVING)

CALORIES: 259

FAT: 20 G

NET CARBS: 3 G

PROTEIN: 1 G

CREAM OF CHICKEN SOUP

INGREDIENTS

7 oz. boneless, skinless chicken breast, chopped

Salt, to taste

½ teaspoon black pepper

½ teaspoon dried oregano

¼ teaspoon cayenne pepper

3 tablespoons unsalted butter

1 tablespoon extra-virgin olive oil

1 scallion, trimmed and chopped

¾ oz. celery, chopped

3 garlic cloves, minced

17.6 oz. chicken stock

7 oz. water

3.5 oz. heavy cream

¼ cup fresh parsley, chopped

1   Season the chicken with salt, pepper, oregano, and cayenne.

2   Place the butter and olive oil in a medium saucepan and warm the mixture over medium heat. Add the scallion whites and celery and cook, stirring occasionally, until they have softened, about 5 minutes.

3   Add the chicken and cook, stirring occasionally, until it is browned all over. Add the garlic and scallion greens and cook, stirring continually, for 1 minute.

4   Add the stock and water and bring the soup to a gentle boil. Taste the soup and adjust the seasoning as necessary.

5   Stir in the cream and parsley. For a thicker soup, simmer the soup until it has reduced and acquired the desired consistency. Ladle the soup into warmed bowls and enjoy.

NUTRITIONAL INFO:
(PER SERVING)

CALORIES: 230

FAT: 21 G

NET CARBS: 6 G

PROTEIN: 4 G

CREAM OF MUSHROOM SOUP

INGREDIENTS

2 tablespoons extra-virgin olive oil

3 tablespoons unsalted butter

2 garlic cloves, minced

4.4 oz. button mushrooms, chopped

4.4 oz. portobello mushrooms, chopped

1 chicken or vegetable bouillon cube

½ teaspoon kosher salt, plus more to taste

½ teaspoon black pepper

¼ teaspoon cayenne pepper

½ teaspoon paprika

10.6 oz. water

3.5 oz. heavy cream

3.5 oz. oyster mushrooms, chopped

1 tablespoon grated Parmesan cheese, for garnish

Fresh basil, chopped, for garnish

1   Place 1 tablespoon of the olive oil and 1 tablespoon of the butter in a medium saucepan and warm the mixture over medium heat. Add the garlic and cook, stirring continually, for 1 minute.

2   Add half of the button and portobello mushrooms and cook, stirring frequently, until they release their liquid, about 2 minutes. Stir in the bouillon cube, salt, pepper, cayenne, and paprika and then add the water. Cook for 2 minutes.

3   Transfer the soup to a blender and puree until smooth. Set the soup aside.

4   Place 1 tablespoon of the butter in the saucepan and melt it over medium heat. Add the remaining button and portobello mushrooms and cook, stirring occasionally, until they release their liquid, about 2 minutes.

5   Strain the soup into the saucepan through a fine sieve and bring it to a simmer. Cook until the mushrooms are cooked through.

6   Stir in the heavy cream, bring the soup back to a simmer, and then remove the pan from heat.

7   Place the remaining butter and olive oil in a large skillet and warm the mixture over medium heat. Add the oyster mushrooms, season them with salt, and cook, stirring occasionally, until they are browned and crispy, 8 to 10 minutes.

8   Ladle the soup into warmed bowls, garnish each portion with 1 teaspoon of the Parmesan and some of the fried oyster mushrooms and basil, and enjoy.

NUTRITIONAL INFO:
(PER SERVING)

CALORIES: 216
FAT: 19 G

NET CARBS: 7 G
PROTEIN: 4 G

CREAM OF SPINACH SOUP

INGREDIENTS

1 tablespoon unsalted butter

1.75 oz. onion, chopped

2 garlic cloves, chopped

5.3 oz. spinach

1 chicken bouillon cube

10.6 oz. water

3.5 oz. heavy cream

Black pepper, to taste

1   Place the butter in a medium saucepan and melt it over medium heat. Add the onion and cook, stirring occasionally, until it is translucent, about 3 minutes. Add the garlic and cook, stirring continually, for 1 minute.

2   Stir in the spinach, bouillon cube, and half of the water. Cover the pan and cook until the spinach wilts, about 2 minutes. Transfer the soup to a blender and puree until smooth.

3   Strain the soup back into the saucepan through a fine sieve, add the remaining water, and bring the soup to a simmer. Stir in the cream and simmer the soup until it has reduced to the desired consistency.

4   Ladle the soup into warmed bowls, sprinkle pepper over each portion, and enjoy.

NUTRITIONAL INFO:
(PER SERVING)

CALORIES: 266
FAT: 26 G

NET CARBS: 5 G
PROTEIN: 2 G

TOMATO SOUP

INGREDIENTS

1.75 oz. salted butter

1.75 oz. onion, chopped

Salt, to taste

2 garlic cloves, chopped

10.6 oz. tomatoes, chopped

Water, as needed

½ teaspoon black pepper, plus more for garnish

½ teaspoon smoked paprika

1 teaspoon pumpkin spice

3.5 oz. chicken stock, plus more as needed

3.5 oz. heavy cream

Fresh basil, chopped, for garnish

Parmesan cheese, grated, for garnish

1. Place the butter in a medium saucepan and melt it over medium heat. Reduce the heat to low, add the onion, and season it with salt. Cook the onion, stirring occasionally, until it starts to caramelize, 12 to 15 minutes.

2. Add the garlic and cook, stirring continually, for 1 minute. Add the tomatoes and cook, stirring frequently, for 2 minutes. Cover the pan and cook for 5 minutes. If the mixture looks too dry, add a bit of water to prevent it from burning.

3. Stir in the pepper, paprika, pumpkin spice, and stock. Cover the pan and cook the soup until the tomatoes have collapsed, about 10 minutes, stirring occasionally.

4. Transfer the soup to a food processor and blitz until it is a smooth puree. Add more stock if a thinner consistency is desired.

5. Strain the soup back into the saucepan through a fine sieve, stir in the cream, and cook the soup until it is warmed through.

6. Ladle the soup into warmed bowls, garnish each portion with pepper, basil, and Parmesan, and enjoy.

SERVINGS: 8   **PREP TIME:** 15 MINUTES   **COOKING TIME:** 7 HOURS

NUTRITIONAL INFO: **CALORIES:** 162   **NET CARBS:** 5 G
(PER SERVING)   **FAT:** 10 G   **PROTEIN:** 14 G

CHICKEN & FENNEL SOUP

INGREDIENTS

16 oz. boneless, skinless chicken thighs, chopped

1 large fennel bulb, trimmed and diced

¼ cup extra-virgin olive oil

½ onion, diced

3 garlic cloves, minced

5 cups chicken stock

4 tomatoes, pureed

2 teaspoons fennel seeds, crushed

Salt and pepper, to taste

1   Place the chicken and fennel in a slow cooker. Set the mixture aside.

2   Place the olive oil in a medium skillet and warm it over medium-high heat. Add the onion and cook, stirring occasionally, until the onion is translucent, about 3 minutes. Add the garlic and cook, stirring continually, for 1 minute. Place the mixture in the slow cooker.

3   Stir the stock, tomatoes, and fennel seeds into the slow cooker, cover it, and cook on low until the chicken is very tender, about 6½ to 7 hours.

4   Season the soup with salt and pepper, ladle it into warmed bowls, and enjoy.

CALAMARI & CHORIZO SALAD

INGREDIENTS

For the Dressing

1.25 oz. feta cheese

¼ cup extra-virgin olive oil

Salt and pepper, to taste

For the Salad

1 tablespoon extra-virgin olive oil

1 tablespoon unsalted butter

3 garlic cloves, chopped

3.5 oz. calamari, rings cut into strips

1 tablespoon Pesto (see page 85)

2 teaspoons Parmesan cheese, grated

1.25 oz. chorizo sausage, crumbled

1.75 oz. mesclun greens

1　To prepare the dressing, place all of the ingredients in a blender and puree until the mixture is rich and creamy. Set the dressing aside.

2　To begin preparations for the salad, place the olive oil and butter in a large skillet and warm the mixture over medium heat. Add the garlic and cook, stirring continually, for 1 minute.

3　Add the calamari, Pesto, and half of the Parmesan, stir to combine, and cook until the calamari is just cooked through, about 2 minutes. Remove the pan from heat and set it aside.

4　Place the chorizo in a separate skillet and cook, stirring occasionally, until it is browned and crispy, about 6 minutes.

5　Place the lettuce and one-third of the dressing in a bowl and toss to combine. Top with the calamari, remaining Parmesan, and chorizo and enjoy.

NUTRITIONAL INFO: CALORIES: 574   NET CARBS: 7 G
(PER SERVING)   FAT: 42 G   PROTEIN: 38 G

SEAFOOD SALAD

INGREDIENTS

1 oz. red onion, sliced

A few drops of fresh lemon juice

2 tablespoons salted butter

2 garlic cloves

Salt and pepper, to taste

2 tablespoons herbes
de Provence

5.3 oz. shrimp, shells removed,
deveined

1 tablespoon mayonnaise

1½ teaspoons sriracha

Fresh dill, to taste

3.5 oz. mixed greens

1 oz. black olives, pits removed,
chopped

1 oz. gherkins, chopped

1 soft-boiled egg, halved

1   Place the onion and lemon juice in a bowl, stir to combine, and let
    the mixture pickle.

2   Place the butter in a large skillet and melt it over medium-low
    heat. Add the garlic, season it with salt, pepper, and the herbes
    de Provence, and cook, stirring continually, for 2 minutes. Add the
    shrimp and cook until they turn pink and are cooked through,
    3 to 6 minutes.

3   Using a slotted spoon, remove the shrimp and garlic from the pan.
    Place the shrimp in a bowl and then grate the garlic into the bowl.

4   Stir in the mayonnaise, sriracha, and the butter that was used to
    sauté the shrimp. Top with the fresh dill and set the mixture aside.

5   Place the pickled onion, lettuce, olives, gherkins, and soft-boiled
    egg in a bowl and toss to combine. Top with the shrimp and enjoy.

NUTRITIONAL INFO:
(PER SERVING)

CALORIES: 466

FAT: 32 G

NET CARBS: 5 G

PROTEIN: 37 G

BEEF & BROCCOLI

INGREDIENTS

1 tablespoon extra-virgin olive oil

1 tablespoon unsalted butter

1 scallion, trimmed and chopped

1 teaspoon grated fresh ginger

1 teaspoon garlic, chopped

5 oz. oyster mushrooms, chopped

8 oz. beef tenderloin, cut into thin strips

Salt and pepper, to taste

Chinese five-spice powder, to taste

½ cup broccoli florets

1 tablespoon rice vinegar

1 tablespoon soy sauce

Sesame seeds, for garnish

1   Place the olive oil and butter in a large skillet and warm the mixture over medium-high heat. Add the scallion whites, ginger, and garlic and stir-fry for 30 seconds. Add the mushrooms and cook, stirring frequently, until they start to brown, 8 to 10 minutes.

2   Add the beef, season it with salt, pepper, and five-spice powder, and cook, stirring frequently, until the beef is browned, about 6 minutes.

3   Place the broccoli in a microwave-safe bowl and microwave on medium for 2 minutes. Add the broccoli to the pan, stir in the rice vinegar, soy sauce, and scallion greens, and stir-fry for 1 minute.

4   Garnish the dish with sesame seeds and enjoy.

SERVINGS: 2   **PREP TIME:** 1 HOUR & 10 MINUTES   **COOKING TIME:** 20 MINUTES

NUTRITIONAL INFO:
(PER SERVING)

CALORIES: 909
FAT: 69 G

NET CARBS: 8 G
PROTEIN: 60 G

CHIPOTLE RIB EYE

INGREDIENTS

2 dried chipotle chile peppers, stems and seeds removed, minced

1 tablespoon dried oregano

1 tablespoon dried cilantro

1 tablespoon black pepper

2 teaspoons cumin

1 teaspoon onion powder

½ teaspoon mustard powder

Salt, to taste

24 oz. rib eye steaks

1 tablespoon extra-virgin olive oil

1 tablespoon chopped fresh parsley, for garnish

Chile peppers, sliced thin, for garnish

1 Place all of the ingredients, except for the steaks and olive oil, in a mixing bowl and stir until well combined.

2 Coat each side of the steaks with some of the olive oil. Generously apply the rub to the steaks and then let them rest at room temperature for 1 hour.

3 Prepare a gas or charcoal grill for medium-high heat (about 450°F).

4 Place the steaks on the grill and cook until the bottoms are nicely seared, about 5 minutes. Turn the steaks over and cook until they have reached the desired level of doneness, about 4 minutes for medium-rare.

5 Remove the steaks from the grill and let them rest for 2 to 3 minutes before garnishing with the parsley and chile peppers and enjoying.

NUTRITIONAL INFO:
(PER SERVING)

CALORIES: 365

FAT: 21 G

NET CARBS: 0 G

PROTEIN: 43 G

FIRE-ROASTED PORK LOIN

INGREDIENTS

5 tablespoons extra-virgin olive oil

2 sprigs of fresh rosemary

36 oz. pork tenderloin

Salt and pepper, to taste

1   Prepare a gas or charcoal grill for medium-low heat (about 350°F). Place the olive oil and rosemary in a cast-iron skillet and warm it over medium heat for 4 to 6 minutes.

2   Season the pork with salt and pepper and place it in the skillet. Turn the pork so that it is evenly coated by the infused oil and sear it over medium heat until it is browned all over.

3   Place the skillet on the grill, cover the grill, and cook the pork for about 30 minutes. Turn the pork and baste it with the pan juices occasionally as it cooks.

4   Remove the pork from the pan and place it directly on the grill. Cook until it is cooked through, turning and basting the pork as needed.

5   Remove the pork from the grill and let it rest for 5 minutes before slicing and serving.

NUTRITIONAL INFO:
(PER SERVING)

CALORIES: 590

FAT: 41 G

NET CARBS: 7 G

PROTEIN: 46 G

PORK VINDALOO

INGREDIENTS

2 tablespoons extra-virgin olive oil

1 large onion, sliced thin

16 oz. tomatoes, diced

6 chile peppers, stems and seeds removed, diced

1 teaspoon turmeric

1 teaspoon coriander

1½ teaspoons garam masala

½ teaspoon cinnamon

40 oz. pork shoulder, trimmed and cubed

10 garlic cloves, peeled

2 tablespoons apple cider vinegar

2 tablespoons grated fresh ginger

1 teaspoon mustard powder

2 cups water

1   Place the olive oil in a medium skillet and warm it over medium-high heat. Add the onion and cook, stirring occasionally, until it is translucent, about 3 minutes.

2   Add the tomatoes, chiles, turmeric, coriander, garam masala, and cinnamon and cook, stirring continually, for 2 minutes. Remove the pan from heat.

3   Place the pork and onion mixture in a slow cooker. Add the remaining ingredients and cook on low until the pork is very tender, 6 to 8 hours.

4   Ladle the vindaloo into warmed bowls and enjoy.

NUTRITIONAL INFO:
(PER SERVING)

CALORIES: 392

FAT: 32 G

NET CARBS: 7 G

PROTEIN: 18 G

LEMON & CAPER SALMON

INGREDIENTS

1 tablespoon extra-virgin olive oil

8.8 oz. salmon fillets, deboned

Salt and pepper, to taste

1.75 oz. red onion, chopped

2.8 oz. unsalted butter

2 garlic cloves, minced

1 tablespoon capers, drained

2 tablespoons chopped
fresh parsley

Fresh lemon juice, to taste

1 Place the olive oil in a large skillet and warm it over medium-high heat. Season the salmon with salt and pepper, place it in the pan, and cook until it is browned on both sides and cooked through, 6 to 8 minutes. Remove the salmon from the pan and cover it loosely with aluminum foil.

2 Add the onion to the pan and cook, stirring occasionally, until it is translucent, about 3 minutes. Reduce the heat to low and add half of the butter. When the butter is melted, add the garlic and capers and cook, stirring continually, for 1 minute.

3 Remove the pan from heat and stir in the remaining butter, parsley, and lemon juice. Pour the sauce over the salmon and enjoy.

NUTRITIONAL INFO:
(PER SERVING)

CALORIES: 470

FAT: 36 G

NET CARBS: 8 G

PROTEIN: 31 G

SHRIMP RISOTTO

INGREDIENTS

2 tablespoons extra-virgin olive oil

3.5 oz. oyster or porcini mushrooms, chopped

1 tablespoon unsalted butter

10.6 oz. Cauliflower Rice (see page 75), uncooked

Salt and pepper, to taste

5.3 oz. fish stock

1 teaspoon dried oregano

½ teaspoon red pepper flakes

8.8 oz. shrimp, shells removed, deveined

3.5 oz. mascarpone cheese

1 tablespoon chopped fresh basil

1   Place 1 tablespoon of the olive oil in a skillet and warm it over medium heat. Add the mushrooms to the skillet and cook, stirring occasionally, until they are browned. Remove the mushrooms from the pan and set them aside.

2   Place the butter and remaining olive oil in the pan and warm the mixture over medium heat. Add the Cauliflower Rice, season it with salt and pepper, and cook for 4 minutes, stirring constantly. Add the stock and cook for another 4 minutes.

3   Season the rice with the oregano and red pepper flakes. Add the shrimp and cook until the rice is tender and the shrimp are cooked through, 3 to 5 minutes.

4   Remove the pan from heat, stir in the mascarpone, basil, mushrooms, and enjoy.

NUTRITIONAL INFO:
(PER SERVING)

CALORIES: 481

FAT: 43 G

NET CARBS: 9 G

PROTEIN: 17 G

MAC & CHEESE

INGREDIENTS

2.1 oz. salted butter

1 small onion, chopped

3.5 oz. ham, chopped

½ teaspoon red pepper flakes

17.6 oz. cauliflower florets

Salt, to taste

½ teaspoon garlic powder

½ teaspoon cayenne pepper

½ teaspoon freshly
grated nutmeg

1 teaspoon fresh thyme

½ chicken bouillon cube

10.6 oz. heavy cream

5.3 oz. cheddar cheese, grated

Black pepper, to taste

¾ oz. pine nuts, crushed

1   Preheat the oven to 390°F. Place half of the butter in a large skillet and melt it over medium heat. Add the onion and cook, stirring occasionally, until it is translucent, about 3 minutes. Add the ham and red pepper flakes and cook, stirring occasionally, until the ham is browned, about 5 minutes. Remove the mixture from the pan and set it aside.

2   Season the cauliflower with salt, place it in a microwave-safe bowl, and microwave on medium for 5 minutes.

3   Place the remaining butter in a saucepan and melt it over medium heat. Stir in the garlic powder, cayenne pepper, nutmeg, thyme, bouillon cube, and cream. Bring the mixture to a simmer and cook until it has reduced by one-quarter.

4   Stir in two-thirds of the cheese and cook until it has melted. Stir the cauliflower and ham mixture into the skillet, season the mixture with pepper, and transfer it to a casserole dish.

5   Top the mac & cheese with the pine nuts and remaining cheese, place it in the oven, and bake for 10 minutes. Place the dish under the broiler and broil until the top of the mac & cheese is crispy and golden brown.

6   Remove the dish from the oven and enjoy.

NUTRITIONAL INFO:
(PER SERVING)

CALORIES: 426
FAT: 38 G

NET CARBS: 7 G
PROTEIN: 15 G

FETTUCCINE ALFREDO

INGREDIENTS

1 tablespoon extra-virgin olive oil

2 mushrooms, chopped

1 garlic clove, grated

3.5 oz. zucchini noodles

1 oz. Parmesan cheese, grated

2 tablespoons heavy cream

½ teaspoon kosher salt

½ teaspoon black pepper

2 thin slices of bacon, cooked
and chopped, for garnish

Fresh parsley, chopped,
for garnish

1 Place the olive oil in a large skillet and warm it over medium heat. Add the mushrooms and cook until the liquid they release has evaporated.

2 Add the garlic and zucchini noodles and cook, stirring continually, for 1 minute.

3 Add the Parmesan and cream and cook, stirring occasionally, until the cheese has melted.

4 Season the dish with salt and pepper, garnish with the bacon and parsley, and enjoy.

NUTRITIONAL INFO:
(PER SERVING)

CALORIES: 516
FAT: 46 G

NET CARBS: 4 G
PROTEIN: 20 G

ZUCCHINI CASSEROLE

INGREDIENTS

3.5 oz. zucchini noodles

2.1 oz. Marinara Sauce
(see page 83)

1 oz. salami, chopped

1 tablespoon extra-virgin olive oil

1.75 oz. mozzarella cheese,
grated

1   Preheat the oven to 390°F. Place the zucchini noodles, sauce, salami, and olive oil in a bowl and stir to combine. Transfer the mixture to a small ovenproof dish and cover it with the cheese.

2   Place the dish in the oven and bake until the cheese is golden brown and the zucchini noodles are tender, 10 to 15 minutes.

3   Remove the casserole from the oven and enjoy.

NUTRITIONAL INFO:
(PER SERVING)

CALORIES: 260
FAT: 19 G

NET CARBS: 5 G
PROTEIN: 14 G

EGGPLANT INVOLTINI

INGREDIENTS

14 oz. eggplant, sliced thin lengthwise

Salt and pepper, to taste

Extra-virgin olive oil, as needed

5.3 oz. ricotta cheese

Red pepper flakes, to taste

1.75 oz. Grana Padano cheese, grated

1 egg

8.8 oz. Marinara Sauce (see page 83)

1.75 oz. mozzarella cheese, grated

Fresh basil, chopped, for garnish

Fresh parsley, chopped, for garnish

1   Preheat the oven to 390°F. Season the eggplant with salt, place it in a colander, and let it sit for 30 minutes.

2   Pat the eggplant dry. Coat a large skillet with olive oil and warm it over medium heat. Add the eggplant and cook until it is browned and just tender, turning the slices as needed. Remove the eggplant from the pan and set it aside.

3   Place the ricotta, salt, pepper, red pepper flakes, Grana Padano, and egg in a mixing bowl and stir to combine. Place 1 tablespoon of the filling at one end of each slice of eggplant and roll the eggplant up lengthwise.

4   Cover the bottom of a casserole dish with some of the sauce. Arrange the stuffed eggplant rolls on top and then top the eggplant with the mozzarella and remaining sauce.

5   Place the dish in the oven and bake until the cheese has melted, about 15 minutes. Remove the dish from the oven, garnish it with basil and parsley, and enjoy.

ASIAN BEEF SALAD

INGREDIENTS

For the Dressing

2 tablespoons extra-virgin olive oil

1 tablespoon natural, no sugar added peanut butter

1 garlic clove, minced

1 teaspoon low-carb soy sauce

1 teaspoon white vinegar

Dash of fish sauce

Juice of 1 lime wedge

2 drops of liquid stevia or preferred keto-friendly sweetener

Salt and pepper, to taste

For the Salad

10.6 oz. beef, sliced into thin strips

Salt, to taste

Curry powder, to taste

1 tablespoon extra-virgin olive oil

1 tablespoon unsalted butter

3.5 oz. enoki mushrooms, chopped

3.5 oz. mesclun greens

Fresh cilantro, chopped, for garnish

1 teaspoon sesame seeds, for garnish

1   To prepare the dressing, place all of the ingredients in a bowl and whisk until the mixture has emulsified. Set the dressing aside.

2   To begin preparations for the salad, season the beef with salt and curry powder. Place the olive oil in a skillet and warm it over medium-high heat. Add the beef and cook until it is done to your liking, turning it as needed. Remove the beef from the pan and place it in a salad bowl.

3   Place the butter in the skillet and melt it over medium heat. Add the mushrooms, season them with salt, and cook, stirring occasionally, until all of the liquid the mushrooms released has evaporated. Add the mushrooms to the salad bowl along with the greens and dressing and toss to combine.

4   Garnish the salad with cilantro and the sesame seeds and enjoy.

NUTRITIONAL INFO:
(PER SERVING)

CALORIES: 465
FAT: 44.1 G

NET CARBS: 6.2 G
PROTEIN: 10.7 G

VEGETARIAN SANDWICHES

INGREDIENTS

¼ cup extra-virgin olive oil

3.75 oz. mushrooms, sliced

1 small red onion, sliced

2 small red bell peppers, stems
and seeds removed, chopped

Salt, to taste

4 oz. baby spinach

8 slices of Cloud Bread
(see page 54)

½ cup mayonnaise

1½ teaspoons Dijon mustard

½ cup microgreens

1   Place half of the olive oil in a skillet and warm it over medium heat.
    Add the mushrooms, onion, and peppers, season the mixture with
    salt, and cook, stirring occasionally, until the vegetables start to
    soften, about 5 minutes. Add the spinach and cook until it has
    wilted, about 2 minutes. Remove the pan from heat.

2   Lightly brush the remaining olive oil on both sides of the slices
    of bread. Place the bread on a baking sheet, place it under the
    broiler, and broil until the tops of the bread are golden brown,
    2 to 3 minutes. Remove the bread from the oven and let it
    cool slightly.

3   Place the mayonnaise and mustard in a small bowl and stir to
    combine. Spread the mixture on the untoasted sides of four slices
    of the bread. Arrange the vegetable mixture and microgreens
    on top of the spread and assemble the sandwiches with the
    remaining slices of bread.

GO FOR THE GREEN SANDWICHES

INGREDIENTS

2 tablespoons extra-virgin olive oil

8 slices of Cloud Bread (see page 54)

6 tablespoons Pesto (see page 85)

7 oz. cherry tomatoes, halved

Flesh of 1 large avocado, sliced

2 oz. baby spinach

½ cup crumbled feta cheese

1 Lightly brush the olive oil on both sides of each slice of bread. Place the bread on a baking sheet, place it under the broiler, and broil until the tops of the bread are golden brown, 2 to 3 minutes. Remove the bread from the oven and let it cool.

2 Spread the Pesto on the untoasted sides of four slices of the bread. Top with the tomatoes, avocado, spinach, and feta and assemble the sandwiches with the remaining pieces of bread.

GO FOR THE GREEN SANDWICHES, SEE PAGE 167

NUTRITIONAL INFO:
(PER SERVING)

CALORIES: 442

FAT: 35 G

NET CARBS: 5 G

PROTEIN: 27 G

CHICKEN SALAD

INGREDIENTS

For the Salad

6.2 oz. boneless, skinless chicken thighs

Salt, to taste

½ teaspoon black pepper

1 teaspoon herbes de Provence

1½ teaspoons apple cider vinegar

1 tablespoon extra-virgin olive oil

1½ teaspoons unsalted butter

3.5 oz. lettuce, sliced

1.75 oz. tomato, sliced

3.5 oz. cucumber, peeled, sliced

1 oz. olives, pits removed, sliced

1.75 oz. feta cheese, crumbled

For the Dressing

1 tablespoon full-fat Greek yogurt

2 tablespoons extra-virgin olive oil

1 teaspoon fresh lemon juice

Salt and pepper, to taste

½ teaspoon cayenne pepper

1   To begin preparations for the salad, place the chicken, salt, pepper, dried herbs, apple cider vinegar, and half of the olive oil in a bowl, stir to combine, and let the mixture marinate for 30 minutes.

2   Place the remaining olive oil in a skillet and warm it over medium heat. Add the chicken and butter and cook until the chicken is cooked through, 3 to 4 minutes per side, frequently basting the chicken with the melted butter as it cooks. Remove the chicken from the pan and set it aside.

3   To prepare the dressing, place all of the ingredients in a mixing bowl and stir until thoroughly combined.

4   Place the vegetables in a bowl and toss until evenly distributed. Slice the chicken, place it on top of the salad, and then sprinkle the feta over everything. Drizzle the dressing over the salad and enjoy.

NUTRITIONAL INFO:
(PER SERVING)

CALORIES: 409

FAT: 32 G

NET CARBS: 2 G

PROTEIN: 28 G

PESTO CHICKEN SALAD

INGREDIENTS

For the Salad

5.3 oz. boneless, skinless chicken thighs

1 teaspoon Italian seasoning

Salt, to taste

1 teaspoon extra-virgin olive oil

½ oz. pine nuts

1 tablespoon bacon fat or unsalted butter

3.5 oz. mesclun greens

1.75 oz. cherry tomatoes, halved

3.5 oz. mozzarella cheese balls

For the Dressing

1 tablespoon Pesto
(see page 85)

2 tablespoons mayonnaise

1   To begin preparations for the salad, place the chicken in a bowl with the Italian seasoning, salt, and olive oil, toss until the chicken is coated, and let it marinate for 10 minutes.

2   Place the pine nuts in a dry skillet and toast over medium heat, shaking the pan frequently, until they are browned, about 2 minutes. Transfer the pine nuts to a salad bowl and let them cool.

3   Place the bacon fat in the skillet and warm it over medium heat. When it is hot, add the chicken and cook until it is cooked through, 3 to 4 minutes per side, turning it as needed. Remove the chicken from the pan and slice it into strips.

4   To prepare the dressing, place all of the ingredients in a small bowl and stir until well combined.

5   Add the chicken, greens, tomatoes, and mozzarella to the salad bowl and toss to combine. Drizzle the dressing over the salad and enjoy.

NUTRITIONAL INFO:
(PER SERVING)

CALORIES: 206
FAT: 16 G

NET CARBS: 6 G
PROTEIN: 6 G

CHORIZO PILAF

INGREDIENTS

1 tablespoon extra-virgin olive oil

1.75 oz. chorizo, diced

½ teaspoon cumin seeds

1 oz. onion, chopped

½ teaspoon grated fresh ginger

½ teaspoon grated garlic

1.75 oz. tomato, chopped

½ teaspoon turmeric

½ teaspoon sweet paprika

Salt, to taste

8.8 oz. Cauliflower Rice
(see page 75)

Fresh cilantro, finely chopped,
for garnish

1   Place the olive oil in a skillet and warm it over medium heat. Add the chorizo and cook, stirring occasionally, until it starts to brown, about 5 minutes. Add the cumin seeds, onion, and ginger and cook, stirring frequently, until the onion is soft, about 8 minutes.

2   Add the garlic, tomato, turmeric, paprika, and a splash of water and cook, stirring occasionally, for 3 to 4 minutes. Season the mixture with salt and add another splash of water. Cook until the sauce has a gravy-like consistency.

3   Stir in the Cauliflower Rice and cook until all of the liquid has evaporated. Garnish with cilantro and serve.

NUTRITIONAL INFO:
(PER SERVING)

CALORIES: 301

FAT: 18 G

NET CARBS: 8 G

PROTEIN: 22 G

CAULIFLOWER PIZZA

INGREDIENTS

8.8 oz. cauliflower florets

Salt and pepper, to taste

½ oz. cream cheese

1 oz. Parmesan cheese, grated

1 egg

2 tablespoons Marinara Sauce (see page 83)

1.75 oz. mozzarella cheese, grated

1 oz. salami, sliced thin

1   Preheat the oven to 375°F and line a baking sheet with parchment paper. Place the cauliflower florets in a food processor and blitz until they are the consistency of couscous. Place the cauliflower in a dry skillet and cook over medium heat, stirring occasionally, until it is browned and tender, 5 to 6 minutes. Place the cauliflower in a kitchen towel, wring the towel to remove as much liquid from the cauliflower as possible, and place the cauliflower in a mixing bowl.

2   Season the cauliflower with salt and pepper, add the cream cheese, Parmesan, and egg, and stir to combine. Place the mixture on the baking sheet and shape it into a circle. Place the pan in the oven and bake for 20 minutes.

3   Remove the pan from the oven and turn the "crust" over. Spread the sauce over the crust and distribute the mozzarella and salami on top. Return the pan to the oven and bake the pizza until the cheese has melted and is starting to brown, about 15 minutes.

4   Remove the pizza from the oven and let it cool briefly before enjoying.

SERVINGS: 2   **PREP TIME:** 5 MINUTES   **COOKING TIME:** 20 MINUTES

NUTRITIONAL INFO:
(PER SERVING)   **CALORIES:** 400   **NET CARBS:** 3 G
                       FAT: 22 G   **PROTEIN:** 49 G

BACON-WRAPPED CHICKEN

INGREDIENTS

2 skinless chicken legs

2 tablespoons plain
full-fat yogurt

1 tablespoon cream cheese

2 garlic cloves, minced

1 oz. mozzarella or cheddar
cheese, grated

Cajun seasoning, to taste

Dried thyme, to taste

Black pepper, to taste

4 slices of bacon

1 Separate the chicken legs into the drumsticks and thighs and score the pieces with a knife.

2 Place the yogurt and cream cheese in a bowl and stir to combine. Add the remaining ingredients, except for the bacon, to the mixture and stir to combine. Place the chicken in the mixture and let it marinate for 1 hour.

3 Preheat the oven to 410°F.

4 Wrap a slice of bacon around each piece of chicken, place the pieces on a baking sheet, and place them in the oven. Bake until the chicken is cooked through and the bacon is crispy, about 20 minutes.

5 Remove the chicken from the oven and let it cool briefly before enjoying.

NUTRITIONAL INFO:
(PER SERVING)

CALORIES: 232
FAT: 12 G

NET CARBS: 0 G
PROTEIN: 32 G

CHICKEN NUGGETS

INGREDIENTS

8.8 oz. boneless, skinless chicken breast

1 teaspoon Old Bay Seasoning

Salt and pepper, to taste

1 egg

Psyllium husk, as needed

Lard or olive oil, as needed

1   Line a baking sheet with parchment paper. Place the chicken, Old Bay Seasoning, salt, and pepper in a food processor and blitz until the mixture is almost a paste. Shape the mixture into nuggets, place them on the parchment-lined baking sheet, and refrigerate for 15 minutes.

2   Place the egg in a bowl, season it with salt, and beat until the egg is scrambled. Place psyllium husk in another bowl. Dip a nugget into the egg and then into the psyllium husk. Repeat until all of the nuggets are completely coated.

3   Add lard or olive oil to a Dutch oven and warm it to 350°F. Add the chicken nuggets and fry until they are browned, crispy, and cooked through, about 8 minutes, turning them as needed.

4   Transfer the fried nuggets to a paper towel–lined plate to drain and cool before enjoying.

NUTRITIONAL INFO:
(PER SERVING)

CALORIES: 477

FAT: 32 G

NET CARBS: 3 G

PROTEIN: 47 G

CHICKEN PARMESAN

INGREDIENTS

10.6 oz. boneless, skinless chicken breast, butterflied

Salt and pepper, to taste

½ egg

1 teaspoon Italian seasoning

1 oz. Parmesan cheese, grated

1 tablespoon finely chopped fresh parsley

1 tablespoon extra-virgin olive oil

1 tablespoon unsalted butter

2 garlic cloves, minced

3.5 oz. tomatoes, pureed

1 teaspoon dried oregano

½ teaspoon red pepper flakes

1 tablespoon fresh basil, minced

3.5 oz. mozzarella cheese, grated

1 Cover the chicken with plastic wrap and pound it thin with a meat tenderizer. Season the chicken with salt and pepper and set it aside.

2 Place the egg and Italian seasoning in a bowl and stir to combine. Combine the Parmesan and parsley in another bowl. Dip the chicken into the egg mixture and then dip it into the Parmesan mixture until it is completely coated.

3 Place the olive oil and half of the butter in a skillet and warm the mixture over medium heat. Add the chicken and cook until it is browned and cooked through, about 2 minutes per side. Remove the chicken from the pan and set it aside.

4 Add the garlic to the skillet and cook, stirring continually, for 1 minute. Add the tomatoes, salt, oregano, red pepper flakes, and remaining butter, cover the pan, and cook the mixture over medium heat for 4 to 5 minutes. Stir in the basil and remove the pan from heat.

5 Preheat the broiler on the oven. Cover the bottom of a baking dish with the tomato sauce, place the chicken on top, and top the chicken with the mozzarella. Broil the chicken until the cheese has melted and is browned, about 5 minutes.

6 Remove the dish from the oven and enjoy.

SERVINGS: 1   **PREP TIME:** 10 MINUTES   **COOKING TIME:** 10 MINUTES

NUTRITIONAL INFO:
(PER SERVING)   **CALORIES:** 563   **NET CARBS:** 2 G
          FAT: 38 G   **PROTEIN:** 39 G

CREAMY PESTO CHICKEN

INGREDIENTS

1 boneless, skinless chicken breast

Salt and pepper, to taste

1 tablespoon extra-virgin olive oil

1.75 oz. water

1 tablespoon Pesto
(see page 85)

1 oz. Parmesan cheese, grated

1.75 oz. heavy cream

1   Cover the chicken with plastic wrap and pound it thin with a meat tenderizer. Season the chicken with salt and pepper and set it aside.

2   Place the olive oil in a skillet and warm it over high heat. Add the chicken and cook until it is browned and cooked through, about 2 minutes per side. Remove the chicken from the pan.

3   Deglaze the pan with the water, scraping up any browned bits from the bottom. Stir in the Pesto, Parmesan, and cream and cook until the sauce is heated through.

4   Stir the resting juices from the chicken into the sauce. Slice the chicken thin, pour the sauce over the top, and enjoy.

FRIED CHICKEN

INGREDIENTS

1 teaspoon kosher salt

1 teaspoon black pepper

1 teaspoon smoked paprika

½ teaspoon cayenne pepper

1 teaspoon garlic powder

4 boneless, skinless chicken breasts

1 egg

3.5 oz. Bread Crumbs (see page 58)

Canola oil, as needed

1 Place the salt, pepper, paprika, cayenne pepper, and garlic powder in a bowl and stir to combine. Dredge the chicken in the mixture until it is completely coated.

2 Place the egg in a bowl and beat it until it is scrambled. Place the Bread Crumbs in another bowl. Dredge the chicken in the egg and then in the Bread Crumbs, repeating until it is completely coated.

3 Add canola oil to a Dutch oven until it is 2 inches deep and warm it to 350°F. Gently slip the chicken into the hot oil and fry until it is golden brown and cooked through, 8 to 10 minutes.

4 Transfer the fried chicken to a paper towel–lined plate to drain and cool before enjoying.

NUTRITIONAL INFO: CALORIES: 271   NET CARBS: 7 G
(PER SERVING)   FAT: 22 G   PROTEIN: 21 G

GARLIC BUTTER CALAMARI

INGREDIENTS

8.8 oz. calamari rings

Salt and pepper, to taste

1.75 oz. salted butter

5 garlic cloves, minced

Pinch of chopped fresh parsley

Pinch of chopped fresh cilantro

1 tablespoon minced scallion

1 teaspoon grated Parmesan cheese

Juice of 1 lemon wedge

1   Season the calamari with salt and pepper and set it aside. Place the butter in a skillet and melt it over medium heat. Add the garlic, parsley, cilantro, and scallion and cook over medium heat, stirring frequently, until the garlic starts to brown, about 2 minutes.

2   Raise the heat to high and add the calamari. Cook, stirring frequently, until the calamari is just cooked through, about 2 minutes.

3   Stir in the Parmesan and lemon juice and enjoy.

SERVINGS: 6
(1 SERVING = 1 FISH CAKE)

PREP TIME: 5 MINUTES

COOKING TIME: 20 MINUTES

NUTRITIONAL INFO:
(PER SERVING)

CALORIES: 149
FAT: 9 G

NET CARBS: 1 G
PROTEIN: 15 G

FISH CAKES

INGREDIENTS

8.4 oz. canned tuna or salmon, drained

1 oz. red onion, diced

2 teaspoons chopped fresh parsley

1 tablespoon mayonnaise

1 teaspoon mustard

1 teaspoon hot sauce

½ teaspoon garlic powder

½ teaspoon paprika

1.75 oz. Bread Crumbs
(see page 58)

Salt and pepper, to taste

2 eggs

1 tablespoon unsalted butter

1 Place all of the ingredients, except for the eggs and butter, in a mixing bowl and stir to combine. Incorporate the eggs and then form the mixture into six cakes.

2 Place the butter in a nonstick skillet and melt it over medium heat. Working in batches to avoid crowding the pan, add the fish cakes and cook until they are browned and cooked through, about 3 to 4 minutes per side. Transfer the cooked fish cakes to a plate and cover loosely with aluminum foil to keep them warm.

NUTRITIONAL INFO:
(PER SERVING)

CALORIES: 452
FAT: 39 G

NET CARBS: 3 G
PROTEIN: 23 G

GARLIC SHRIMP

INGREDIENTS

3.5 oz. shrimp, shells removed, deveined

¼ teaspoon kosher salt

¼ teaspoon black pepper

¼ teaspoon cayenne pepper

½ teaspoon dried oregano

1 tablespoon extra-virgin olive oil

2 tablespoons unsalted butter

2 garlic cloves, minced

1 tablespoon chopped fresh parsley

Juice of ½ lemon

1. Place the shrimp, salt, pepper, cayenne, and oregano in a bowl and toss to combine. Let the shrimp marinate in the refrigerator for 30 minutes.

2. Place the olive oil and 1 tablespoon of the butter in a skillet and warm the mixture over medium heat. Add the garlic and parsley and cook, stirring continually, for 1 minute.

3. Add the shrimp and cook until they turn pink and are cooked through, 3 to 5 minutes.

4. Remove the pan from heat, stir in the remaining butter and the lemon juice, and enjoy.

NUTRITIONAL INFO:
(PER SERVING)

CALORIES: 326

FAT: 25 G

NET CARBS: 0 G

PROTEIN: 22 G

TUNA SALAD

INGREDIENTS

3.5 oz. cabbage, shredded

¼ cup mayonnaise

2 tablespoons horseradish sauce

2 slices of bacon, cooked
and chopped

Salt and pepper, to taste

4 hard-boiled eggs

7 oz. canned tuna, drained

¾ oz. celery, diced

¾ oz. scallions, diced

¾ oz. lettuce, diced

¾ oz. green bell pepper, diced

1 teaspoon mustard

1 teaspoon sriracha

1   Place the cabbage, half of the mayonnaise and horseradish sauce, and the bacon in a bowl, season the mixture with salt and pepper, and stir to combine. Set the mixture aside.

2   Chop two of the eggs, place them in a bowl, add the tuna, and stir to combine. Add the remaining ingredients, along with the remaining mayonnaise and horseradish sauce, and stir to combine.

3   Incorporate the cabbage mixture, cut the remaining eggs in half, place them on top of the salad, and enjoy.

NUTRITIONAL INFO:
(PER SERVING)

CALORIES: 417
FAT: 26 G

NET CARBS: 1 G
PROTEIN: 36 G

MEATZA

INGREDIENTS

8.8 oz. ground chicken

Salt and pepper, to taste

1 teaspoon garlic powder

1 teaspoon extra-virgin olive oil

1 tablespoon Pesto
(see page 85)

⅓ oz. mushrooms, sliced

2.6 oz. mozzarella cheese, grated

¾ oz. pepperoni

1   Place the ground chicken in a bowl and season it with salt, pepper, and the garlic powder. Stir to combine and set the mixture aside.

2   Place the olive oil in a cast-iron skillet and warm it over medium heat. Form the chicken into a ½-inch-thick round and add it to the pan. Cook the chicken until it is browned and almost cooked through, 6 to 8 minutes.

3   Preheat the oven's broiler. Remove the pan from heat, spread the Pesto over the "pizza," and then top it with the mushrooms, cheese, and pepperoni.

4   Place the skillet under the broiler and broil until the cheese has melted and is browned and the pizza is completely cooked through.

5   Remove the pizza from the oven and enjoy immediately.

NUTRITIONAL INFO:
(PER SERVING)

CALORIES: 274
FAT: 18 G

NET CARBS: 6 G
PROTEIN: 20 G

PORK FRIED RICE

INGREDIENTS

1 tablespoon extra-virgin olive oil

1 tablespoon unsalted butter

1 scallion, trimmed and chopped

8.8 oz. ground pork

2 garlic cloves, chopped

1 teaspoon kosher salt

½ teaspoon black pepper

½ teaspoon paprika

¼ teaspoon cayenne pepper

1 teaspoon dried oregano

½ teaspoon red pepper flakes

3.5 oz. bell peppers, chopped

7 oz. baby spinach

17.6 oz. Cauliflower Rice
(see page 75)

1.75 oz. cheddar cheese, grated

1 oz. heavy cream

8 olives, pits removed, chopped

Fresh parsley, chopped,
for garnish

Parmesan cheese, grated,
for garnish

1. Place the olive oil and butter in a large skillet and warm the mixture over medium heat. Add the scallion whites and the ground pork and cook, while breaking the pork up with a wooden spoon, until the pork starts to brown, about 8 minutes.

2. Stir in the garlic, salt, pepper, paprika, cayenne pepper, oregano, red pepper flakes, bell peppers, and spinach and stir-fry until the spinach has wilted, about 2 minutes.

3. Stir in the Cauliflower Rice, cheddar cheese, heavy cream, and scallion greens. Cook for 1 minute, stir in the olives, garnish the dish with parsley and Parmesan, and enjoy.

DESSERTS

Left to their own devices, many people actually think about dessert first, and then work backward to decide what should precede it. For these folks, the thought of following any diet that yanks the sweet tooth out of their mouth is unthinkable. For them, there's some great news: it's easy to enjoy luscious desserts while strictly following a keto diet. The secret to keto desserts is swapping out ingredients such as wheat flour and traditional sweeteners that are rife with carbs. Just one thing: keep in mind that low-carb baked goods will be similar to those made with wheat flour and sugar, but they won't be identical. There will be differences in taste and texture. But the end result can be just as satisfying.

NUTRITIONAL INFO:
(PER SERVING)

CALORIES: 152

FAT: 11.8 G

NET CARBS: 3.5 G

PROTEIN: 8.7 G

LAVA CAKES

INGREDIENTS

Canola oil, as needed

¼ cup heavy cream

4 large eggs

½ teaspoon kosher salt

1 teaspoon baking powder

1 teaspoon pure vanilla extract

½ cup unsweetened cocoa powder

½ cup granulated erythritol or preferred keto-friendly sweetener

1   Preheat the oven to 350°F and coat four ramekins with canola oil. Place the cream, eggs, salt, baking powder, and vanilla in a bowl and whisk until combined. Stir in the cocoa powder and erythritol and divide the mixture among the ramekins.

2   Place the ramekins in the oven and bake until the cakes are just set, 10 to 12 minutes. Place a plate over the top of each ramekin, invert it, and tap on a counter to release the cake. Enjoy immediately.

NUTRITIONAL INFO:
(PER SERVING)

CALORIES: 213

FAT: 16.6 G

NET CARBS: 8.7 G

PROTEIN: 6.1 G

NO-BAKE BLUEBERRY CHEESECAKE

INGREDIENTS

3.75 oz. raw cashews

2 oz. unsweetened shredded coconut

2 tablespoons coconut oil

7 oz. blueberries

2 tablespoons beet juice

¼ cup stevia or preferred keto-friendly sweetener

1 tablespoon water

1 (14 oz.) can of coconut milk, chilled

2 cups full-fat Greek yogurt

8.5 oz. firm silken tofu

1   Line a springform pan with parchment paper and coat the paper with nonstick cooking spray. Place two-thirds of the cashews, the coconut, and coconut oil in a food processor and pulse until the mixture is coarse crumbs. Press the mixture into the base of the springform pan and chill it in the refrigerator.

2   Place three-quarters of the blueberries, the beet juice, sweetener, and water in a saucepan, cover the pan, and cook over medium heat until the berries are soft and juicy, about 6 to 8 minutes. Transfer the mixture to a blender and puree until smooth.

3   Strain the puree through a fine sieve into a mixing bowl. Place the coconut milk, yogurt, and tofu in a separate mixing bowl and whisk until the mixture is smooth. Scrape both mixtures on top of the base in the springform pan and gently stir with a rubber spatula until the mixture is swirled. Chill the cheesecake in the refrigerator for 4 hours.

4   Crush the remaining cashews. Sprinkle them and the remaining blueberries over the cheesecake and enjoy.

NUTRITIONAL INFO: (PER SERVING OF CAKE)	CALORIES: 218 FAT: 17 G	NET CARBS: 3 G PROTEIN: 5 G
(PER SERVING OF GANACHE)	CALORIES: 156 FAT: 21 G	NET CARBS: 1 G PROTEIN: 3 G

VANILLA MUG CAKE

INGREDIENTS

For the Cake

1 oz. coconut flour

2 tablespoons unsalted butter

2 teaspoons coconut milk

½ teaspoon pure vanilla extract

¼ teaspoon baking powder

1 egg

Stevia or preferred keto-friendly sweetener, to taste

Pinch of kosher salt

For the Ganache

1½ teaspoons unsalted butter or cocoa butter

1½ teaspoons natural, no sugar added peanut butter

½ teaspoon unsweetened cocoa powder

Stevia or preferred keto-friendly sweetener, to taste

½ teaspoon coconut milk

1   To prepare the cake, combine all of the ingredients in a large mug, place the mug in the microwave, and microwave on high for 1½ minutes. Remove the mug from the microwave, turn the mug over, and tap it until the cake falls out.

2   To prepare the ganache, place the butter and peanut butter in a microwave-safe bowl and microwave on medium for 30 seconds. Remove and stir to combine. Add the cocoa powder, sweetener, and coconut milk and stir until thoroughly combined. Drizzle half of the ganache over the cake and enjoy.

NUTRITIONAL INFO:
(PER SERVING)

CALORIES: 178
FAT: 16.5 G

NET CARBS: 5.1 G
PROTEIN: 2.5 G

CHOCOLATE CHIP COOKIES

INGREDIENTS

1 cup unsalted butter

1½ cups almond flour

½ cup coconut flour

1½ teaspoons baking soda

2 tablespoons coconut oil, melted

½ cup stevia or preferred keto-friendly sweetener

2 teaspoons pure vanilla extract

8 oz. sugar-free semisweet chocolate chips

1   Preheat the oven to 350°F and line two baking sheets with parchment paper. Place the butter in a saucepan and cook it over medium-high heat until it is dark brown and has a nutty aroma. Transfer the browned butter to a heatproof mixing bowl and set it aside.

2   Place the flours and baking soda in a mixing bowl and whisk until combined. Set the mixture aside.

3   Add the coconut oil, sweetener, and vanilla to the bowl containing the melted butter and whisk until combined. Gradually add the dry mixture and stir until the mixture comes together as a dough. Add the chocolate chips and fold until evenly distributed. Form tablespoons of the mixture into balls and place them on the parchment-lined baking sheets, leaving about 2 inches between each ball. Gently press down on the balls to flatten them slightly.

4   Place the cookies in the oven and bake, rotating the sheets halfway through, until they are golden brown, about 12 minutes. Remove the cookies from the oven and let them cool on the baking sheets for 10 minutes before transferring to wire racks to cool completely.

PEANUT BUTTER COOKIES

INGREDIENTS

½ cup salted, no sugar added peanut butter

1 tablespoon coconut oil, melted

⅓ cup stevia or preferred keto-friendly sweetener

1 cup almond flour

¾ teaspoon baking soda

1 teaspoon pure vanilla extract

½ teaspoon flaky sea salt

1 Preheat the oven to 350°F and line a large baking sheet with parchment paper. Place all of the ingredients, except for the salt, in a mixing bowl and stir to combine.

2 Drop tablespoons of the dough on the baking sheet, gently press down to flatten them, and then press down on them with a fork to leave a crosshatch pattern on top.

3 Place the cookies in the oven and bake until the edges are set and golden brown, about 10 minutes. Remove the cookies from the oven and let them cool on the baking sheet for 10 minutes before transferring to a wire rack to cool completely.

4 Sprinkle the salt over the cookies and enjoy.

NUTRITIONAL INFO:
(PER SERVING)

CALORIES: 117

FAT: 10.6 G

NET CARBS: 4.5 G

PROTEIN: 3.7 G

ALMOND CLOUDS

INGREDIENTS

4 tablespoons unsalted butter, softened

2 oz. cream cheese, at room temperature

⅓ cup monk fruit sweetener

1 large egg

1 tablespoon sour cream

1½ teaspoons pure almond extract

½ teaspoon pure vanilla extract

Pinch of kosher salt

3 cups almond flour

24 blanched almonds

1 Preheat the oven to 350°F and line two baking sheets with parchment paper. Place the butter, cream cheese, and sweetener in the work bowl of a stand mixer fitted with the paddle attachment and beat at medium speed until light and fluffy. Add the egg, sour cream, extracts, and salt and beat until well combined.

2 Reduce the mixer's speed to low and incorporate the almond flour ½ cup at a time.

3 Form 1½-tablespoon portions of the dough into balls and place them on the baking sheets, making sure to leave about 2 inches between the cookies. Gently press down on the cookies to flatten them and press an almond into the center of each one.

4 Place the cookies in the oven and bake until the edges are set and lightly browned, about 15 minutes. Remove the cookies from the oven and let them cool on the baking sheets before enjoying.

NUTRITIONAL INFO:
(PER SERVING)

CALORIES: 96

FAT: 9 G

NET CARBS: 2.1 G

PROTEIN: 2.4 G

COCONUT MACAROONS

INGREDIENTS

8.4 oz. unsweetened shredded coconut

5 large egg whites, at room temperature

½ teaspoon cream of tartar

¼ teaspoon kosher salt

½ cup granulated erythritol

½ cup powdered erythritol

1 teaspoon pure vanilla extract

1 Preheat the oven to 350°F and line two baking sheets with parchment paper. Place the coconut on another baking sheet, place it in the oven, and toast the coconut until it is lightly browned, 7 to 10 minutes. Remove the coconut from the oven and let it cool. Reduce the oven temperature to 275°F.

2 Place the egg whites in a mixing bowl and beat them with a handheld mixer until frothy. Add the cream of tartar and salt and beat until the mixture holds soft peaks. Incorporate both forms of erythritol a tablespoon at a time and beat until the mixture holds stiff peaks. Stir in the vanilla and then fold the toasted coconut into the meringue.

3 Drop heaping tablespoons of the meringue onto the parchment-lined baking sheets, leaving about 1½ inches between each portion.

4 Place the macaroons in the oven and bake until they are dry to the touch. Remove the cookies from the oven and place the baking sheets on wire racks to cool.

NUTRITIONAL INFO: **CALORIES:** 244   **NET CARBS:** 11.8 G
(PER SERVING)   **FAT:** 20.3 G   **PROTEIN:** 2.6 G

DARK CHOCOLATE & STOUT BROWNIES

INGREDIENTS

1 cup unsalted butter,
plus more as needed

1¼ cups Guinness

11 oz. sugar-free chocolate chips

3 large eggs

1 teaspoon pure vanilla extract

¾ cup almond flour

1 teaspoon kosher salt

¼ cup unsweetened cocoa
powder

1   Preheat the oven to 350°F and coat an 8-inch square cake pan with butter. Place the stout in a medium saucepan, bring it to a boil, and cook until it has reduced by half. Remove the pan from heat and let the stout cool.

2   Place the chocolate chips and butter in a microwave-safe bowl and microwave on medium until melted, removing to stir every 15 seconds.

3   Place the eggs and vanilla in a large mixing bowl and whisk until combined. Slowly whisk in the chocolate-and-butter mixture and then whisk in the reduced stout. Add the almond flour and salt and fold the mixture until it comes together as a smooth batter. Pour the batter into the pan.

4   Place the brownies in the oven and bake until the surface begins to crack and a toothpick inserted into the center comes out with a few moist crumbs attached, about 35 minutes. Remove the brownies from the oven and let them cool in the pan.

5   Sprinkle the cocoa powder over the brownies, cut them into squares, and enjoy.

COFFEE & CHOCOLATE TARTS

INGREDIENTS

1.5 oz. almond flour

1 teaspoon unsweetened cocoa powder

Stevia or preferred keto-friendly sweetener, to taste

1 teaspoon pure vanilla extract

2 tablespoons salted butter, melted

1 teaspoon instant espresso powder

2 tablespoons hot water (125°F)

5.3 oz. mascarpone cheese

3.5 oz. heavy cream

1 oz. 85 percent dark chocolate

Coarse sea salt, to taste

1. Preheat the oven to 350°F. Place the almond flour, cocoa powder, sweetener, vanilla, and butter in a mixing bowl and stir until the mixture has the consistency of wet sand.

2. Divide the mixture among three ramekins and press it into their bases until it is smooth and even. Place the ramekins in the oven and bake the bases for 10 minutes. Remove the bases from the oven and let them cool slightly.

3. Dissolve the instant espresso powder in the hot water and let it cool.

4. Place the mascarpone cheese, more sweetener, and the espresso in a bowl and beat until the mixture is nice and fluffy. Pour the mascarpone mixture over the cooled tart bases and refrigerate the tarts for 10 minutes.

5. Place the heavy cream in a microwave-safe bowl and microwave on medium for 30 seconds. Add the chocolate and more sweetener and stir until you have a creamy ganache. Pour the ganache over the tarts and refrigerate for 1 hour.

6. Sprinkle sea salt over the tarts and enjoy.

NUTRITIONAL INFO:
(PER SERVING)

CALORIES: 311

FAT: 29.6 G

NET CARBS: 6.8 G

PROTEIN: 5.2 G

CHOCOLATE ICE CREAM

INGREDIENTS

1½ cups heavy cream

¾ cup whole milk

¼ cup unsweetened cocoa powder

½ cup stevia or preferred keto-friendly sweetener

3 large egg yolks, lightly beaten

1.75 oz. Baker's Chocolate, chopped

½ teaspoon pure vanilla extract

Pinch of flaky sea salt

1½ tablespoons vodka (optional)

1. Prepare an ice bath in a large bowl. Place the cream, ½ cup of the milk, the cocoa powder, and sweetener in a saucepan and warm the mixture over medium heat, stirring continually. Once the sweetener has dissolved, take approximately 1 cup from the mixture in the saucepan and whisk it into the bowl containing the egg yolks. Add the tempered egg yolks to the saucepan and continue cooking over medium heat, stirring continually, until the custard has thickened to where it will coat the back of a wooden spoon. Remove the pan from heat.

2. Stir the chocolate into the custard, let the mixture cool for 5 minutes, and then stir until it is smooth. Pour the custard into a metal bowl and then set the bowl in the ice bath. Stir occasionally until the mixture is smooth, about 10 minutes. Cover the bowl with plastic wrap and refrigerate for 3 hours.

3. Stir the remaining milk, the vanilla, salt, and vodka (if using) into the chilled custard. Pour the custard into an ice cream maker and churn until the ice cream has the desired consistency, about 20 minutes. Pour the ice cream into an airtight container, cover, and freeze until firm, about 4 hours.

TIPS: Using the vodka will help prevent the formation of ice crystals in the ice cream without affecting the flavor, ultimately yielding a smoother texture.

MCT OIL

MCT oil is a dietary supplement that is made up of medium-chain triglycerides, meaning they are composed of chains of 6 to 12 carbon atoms. They are processed differently than other fats, going straight from the gut to the liver, where they are turned into the ketones that the ketogenic diet aims to produce.

NUTRITIONAL INFO:
(PER SERVING)

CALORIES: 259
FAT: 24.5 G

NET CARBS: 3 G
PROTEIN: 2.9 G

AVOCADO ICE CREAM

INGREDIENTS

Flesh of 2 avocados

1 cup coconut milk

1 tablespoon fresh lemon juice

1 tablespoon MCT oil

2 tablespoons stevia or preferred keto-friendly sweetener

Pinch of kosher salt

Unsweetened coconut flakes, toasted, for garnish

1 Place the avocados, coconut milk, lemon juice, MCT oil, sweetener, and salt in a food processor and puree until smooth, scraping down the sides of the work bowl as needed.

2 Transfer the mixture to an ice cream maker and churn until the ice cream has the desired consistency, about 20 minutes. Transfer the mixture to an airtight container, cover, and freeze for 4 hours.

3 To serve, garnish each portion with some coconut.

NUTRITIONAL INFO:
(PER SERVING)

CALORIES: 153
FAT: 12 G

NET CARBS: 7 G
PROTEIN: 5.2 G

CHOCOLATE PUDDING

INGREDIENTS

¼ cup stevia or preferred keto-friendly sweetener

1.25 oz. Baker's Chocolate, grated

¼ cup unsweetened cocoa powder

¼ cup almond flour

½ teaspoon kosher salt

2 cups whole milk

¼ cup heavy cream

4 tablespoons unsalted butter, divided into tablespoons

2 teaspoons pure vanilla extract

¾ oz. unsweetened shredded coconut (optional)

2.5 oz. raspberries (optional)

1.25 oz. sugar-free chocolate, grated (optional)

1. Place the sweetener, chocolate, cocoa powder, almond flour, and salt in a saucepan and whisk to combine. Cook over medium heat and slowly add the milk, whisking continually. Cook until the mixture thickens and comes to a boil, approximately 8 to 10 minutes.

2. Reduce the heat to low and simmer the mixture for 1 to 2 minutes. Remove the saucepan from heat and stir in the cream.

3. Incorporate the butter 1 tablespoon at a time and then stir in the vanilla.

4. Transfer the pudding into the serving dishes and place plastic wrap directly on the surface to prevent a skin from forming. Refrigerate the pudding for 2 hours before serving and top with the shredded coconut, raspberries, and/or chocolate shavings, if desired.

NUTRITIONAL INFO:
(PER SERVING)

CALORIES: 146
FAT: 14 G

NET CARBS: 2 G
PROTEIN: 3 G

ETON MESS

INGREDIENTS

2 egg whites

¼ teaspoon cream of tartar

1 teaspoon pure vanilla extract

1½ teaspoons powdered erythritol

5.3 oz. heavy cream

Stevia or preferred keto-friendly sweetener, to taste

3.5 oz. strawberries, hulled and diced

1   Preheat the oven to 245°F and line a baking sheet with parchment paper. Place the egg whites in a bowl and beat until they are frothy. Add the cream of tartar and beat until the mixture holds soft peaks. Add half of the vanilla and the erythritol and whisk to combine.

2   Transfer the meringue to the baking sheet and bake until it is cooked through and dry to the touch, 30 to 35 minutes. Remove the meringue from the oven and let the meringue cool for 15 minutes before removing it from the parchment paper.

3   While the meringue is in the oven, place the cream, sweetener, and remaining vanilla in a bowl and beat until the mixture holds soft peaks. Refrigerate for 15 minutes and then fold the strawberries into the mixture. Break the meringue into pieces, add it to the strawberries and cream, and serve.

NUTRITIONAL INFO: **CALORIES:** 199   **NET CARBS:** 1.5 G
(PER SERVING)   **FAT:** 18.9 G   **PROTEIN:** 3 G

CHIA & SESAME BLISS BALLS

INGREDIENTS

½ cup coconut oil, melted

½ cup coconut butter, melted

¼ cup unsweetened cocoa powder

1 teaspoon pure almond extract

½ teaspoon pure vanilla extract

½ teaspoon liquid stevia or preferred keto-friendly sweetener

2.8 oz. white chia seeds

2 tablespoons sesame seeds

1   Place the coconut oil and coconut butter in a bowl and stir to combine. Stir in the cocoa powder, extracts, and sweetener, cover the bowl, and freeze until the mixture is set, about 20 minutes.

2   Combine the chia seeds and sesame seeds in a shallow dish. Form 2-tablespoon portions of the coconut mixture into balls and roll them in the seed mixture until completely coated. Enjoy immediately or store in the refrigerator.

NUTRITIONAL INFO:
(PER SERVING)

CALORIES: 212

FAT: 20.7 G

NET CARBS: 4.3 G

PROTEIN: 3 G

COCONUT BLISS BALLS

INGREDIENTS

½ cup coconut oil, melted

½ cup almond butter, melted

2 tablespoons real maple syrup

3.2 oz. unsweetened
shredded coconut

1.75 oz. almonds, chopped

½ teaspoon pure vanilla extract

Pinch of kosher salt

1   Place the coconut oil, almond butter, and maple syrup in a bowl and stir to combine. Stir in two-thirds of the coconut, the almonds, vanilla, and salt, cover the bowl, and freeze the mixture until it is set, about 20 minutes.

2   Place the remaining coconut in a shallow dish. Form 2-tablespoon portions of the almond butter mixture into balls and roll them in the coconut until completely coated. Enjoy immediately or store in the refrigerator.

COCONUT BLISS BALLS, SEE PAGE 229

NUTRITIONAL INFO:
(PER SERVING)

CALORIES: 308
FAT: 29 G

NET CARBS: 5 G
PROTEIN: 16 G

TIRAMISU

INGREDIENTS

2.1 oz. brewed espresso

1 oz. whiskey (optional)

1 oz. heavy cream

1 egg, yolk and white separated

Stevia or preferred keto-friendly sweetener, to taste

14 oz. mascarpone cheese

2 portions of Mug Bread (see page 57)

2 teaspoons unsweetened cocoa powder

1 Place the espresso, whiskey (if using), and cream in a bowl and stir to combine. Place the egg white in a bowl and whisk until it holds stiff peaks. Set both aside.

2 Place the egg yolk and sweetener in a separate bowl and whisk until the mixture is a pale yellow. Add the mascarpone cheese and 2.1 oz. of the espresso mixture and whisk until the mixture is a smooth custard. Working in two batches, fold in the beaten egg white.

3 Slice the bread as desired and then dip the slices into the remaining espresso mixture. Layer them in the dish, pour the custard over the top, and refrigerate until set, about 10 minutes. Dust the tiramisu with the cocoa powder before serving.

METRIC CONVERSIONS

US Measurement	Approximate Metric Liquid Measurement	Approximate Metric Dry Measurement
1 teaspoon	5 ml	5 g
1 tablespoon or ½ ounce	15 ml	14 g
1 ounce or ⅛ cup	30 ml	29 g
¼ cup or 2 ounces	60 ml	57 g
⅓ cup	80 ml	76 g
½ cup or 4 ounces	120 ml	113 g
⅔ cup	160 ml	151 g
¾ cup or 6 ounces	180 ml	170 g
1 cup or 8 ounces or ½ pint	240 ml	227 g
1½ cups or 12 ounces	350 ml	340 g
2 cups or 1 pint or 16 ounces	475 ml	454 g
3 cups or 1½ pints	700 ml	680 g
4 cups or 2 pints or 1 quart	950 ml	908 g

INDEX

ABOUT CIDER MILL PRESS BOOK PUBLISHERS

Good ideas ripen with time. From seed to harvest, Cider Mill Press brings fine reading, information, and entertainment together between the covers of its creatively crafted books. Our Cider Mill bears fruit twice a year, publishing a new crop of titles each spring and fall.

"Where Good Books Are Ready for Press"

Visit us online at
cidermillpress.com

or write to us at
PO Box 454
12 Spring St.
Kennebunkport, Maine 04046